JUL 2 2 1992

J
B
LEE, R. E.

ROBERT E. LEE

ROBERT E. LEE

Warren Brown

CHELSEA HOUSE PUBLISHERS
NEW YORK
PHILADELPHIA

Chelsea House Publishers
EDITOR-IN-CHIEF: Remmel Nunn
MANAGING EDITOR: Karyn Gullen Browne
COPY CHIEF: Mark Rifkin
PICTURE EDITOR: Adrian G. Allen
ART DIRECTOR: Maria Epes
ASSISTANT ART DIRECTOR: Noreen Romano
MANUFACTURING MANAGER: Gerald Levine
SYSTEMS MANAGER: Lindsey Ottman
PRODUCTION MANAGER: Joseph Romano
PRODUCTION COORDINATOR: Marie Claire Cebrián

World Leaders—Past & Present
SENIOR EDITOR: John W. Selfridge

Staff for ROBERT E. LEE
COPY EDITOR: Joseph Roman
EDITORIAL ASSISTANT: Martin Mooney
PICTURE RESEARCHER: Lisa Kirchner
DESIGNER: David Murray
ASSISTANT DESIGNER: Diana Blume
COVER ILLUSTRATION: Robert Caputo

First Printing

1 3 5 7 9 8 6 4 2

Library of Congress Cataloging-in-Publication Data

Brown, Warren.
   Robert E. Lee/Warren Brown.
      p.   cm.—(World leaders past & present)
   Includes bibliographical references and index.
   Summary: Chronicles the life and times of the Civil War general who
commanded the Confederate Army.
   ISBN 1-55546-814-4
      0-7910-1462-2 (pbk.)
   1. Lee, Robert E. (Robert Edward), 1807–70—Juvenile literature.
2. Generals—United States—Biography—Juvenile literature.
3. United States. Army—Biography—Juvenile literature.
4. Confederate States of America. Army—Biography—Juvenile
literature.   5. United States—History—Civil War, 1861–65—
Campaigns—Juvenile literature.   [1. Lee, Robert E. (Robert Edward),
1807–70. 2. Generals. 3. Confederate States of America. Army—
Biography. 4. United States—History—Civil War, 1861–65.]
I. Title. II. Series.
E467.1.L4B86   1991   91-10643
973.7′3′092—dc20   CIP
[B]   AC

Contents

JOHN ADAMS
JOHN QUINCY ADAMS
KONRAD ADENAUER
ALEXANDER THE GREAT
SALVADOR ALLENDE
MARC ANTONY
CORAZON AQUINO
YASIR ARAFAT
KING ARTHUR
HAFEZ AL-ASSAD
KEMAL ATATÜRK
ATTILA
CLEMENT ATTLEE
AUGUSTUS CAESAR
MENACHEM BEGIN
DAVID BEN-GURION
OTTO VON BISMARCK
LÉON BLUM
SIMON BOLÍVAR
CESARE BORGIA
WILLY BRANDT
LEONID BREZHNEV
JULIUS CAESAR
JOHN CALVIN
JIMMY CARTER
FIDEL CASTRO
CATHERINE THE GREAT
CHARLEMAGNE
CHIANG KAI-SHEK
WINSTON CHURCHILL
GEORGES CLEMENCEAU
CLEOPATRA
CONSTANTINE THE GREAT
HERNÁN CORTÉS
OLIVER CROMWELL
GEORGES-JACQUES
    DANTON
JEFFERSON DAVIS
MOSHE DAYAN
CHARLES DE GAULLE
EAMON DE VALERA
EUGENE DEBS
DENG XIAOPING
BENJAMIN DISRAELI
ALEXANDER DUBČEK
FRANÇOIS & JEAN-CLAUDE
    DUVALIER
DWIGHT EISENHOWER
ELEANOR OF AQUITAINE
ELIZABETH I
FAISAL
FERDINAND & ISABELLA
FRANCISCO FRANCO
BENJAMIN FRANKLIN

FREDERICK THE GREAT
INDIRA GANDHI
MOHANDAS GANDHI
GIUSEPPE GARIBALDI
AMIN & BASHIR GEMAYEL
GENGHIS KHAN
WILLIAM GLADSTONE
MIKHAIL GORBACHEV
ULYSSES S. GRANT
ERNESTO "CHE" GUEVARA
TENZIN GYATSO
ALEXANDER HAMILTON
DAG HAMMARSKJÖLD
HENRY VIII
HENRY OF NAVARRE
PAUL VON HINDENBURG
HIROHITO
ADOLF HITLER
HO CHI MINH
KING HUSSEIN
IVAN THE TERRIBLE
ANDREW JACKSON
JAMES I
WOJCIECH JARUZELSKI
THOMAS JEFFERSON
JOAN OF ARC
POPE JOHN XXIII
POPE JOHN PAUL II
LYNDON JOHNSON
BENITO JUÁREZ
JOHN KENNEDY
ROBERT KENNEDY
JOMO KENYATTA
AYATOLLAH KHOMEINI
NIKITA KHRUSHCHEV
KIM IL SUNG
MARTIN LUTHER KING, JR.
HENRY KISSINGER
KUBLAI KHAN
LAFAYETTE
ROBERT E. LEE
VLADIMIR LENIN
ABRAHAM LINCOLN
DAVID LLOYD GEORGE
LOUIS XIV
MARTIN LUTHER
JUDAS MACCABEUS
JAMES MADISON
NELSON & WINNIE
    MANDELA
MAO ZEDONG
FERDINAND MARCOS
GEORGE MARSHALL

MARY, QUEEN OF SCOTS
TOMÁŠ MASARYK
GOLDA MEIR
KLEMENS VON METTERNICH
JAMES MONROE
HOSNI MUBARAK
ROBERT MUGABE
BENITO MUSSOLINI
NAPOLÉON BONAPARTE
GAMAL ABDEL NASSER
JAWAHARLAL NEHRU
NERO
NICHOLAS II
RICHARD NIXON
KWAME NKRUMAH
DANIEL ORTEGA
MOHAMMED REZA PAHLAVI
THOMAS PAINE
CHARLES STEWART
    PARNELL
PERICLES
JUAN PERÓN
PETER THE GREAT
POL POT
MUAMMAR EL-QADDAFI
RONALD REAGAN
CARDINAL RICHELIEU
MAXIMILIEN ROBESPIERRE
ELEANOR ROOSEVELT
FRANKLIN ROOSEVELT
THEODORE ROOSEVELT
ANWAR SADAT
HAILE SELASSIE
PRINCE SIHANOUK
JAN SMUTS
JOSEPH STALIN
SUKARNO
SUN YAT-SEN
TAMERLANE
MOTHER TERESA
MARGARET THATCHER
JOSIP BROZ TITO
TOUSSAINT L'OUVERTURE
LEON TROTSKY
PIERRE TRUDEAU
HARRY TRUMAN
QUEEN VICTORIA
LECH WALESA
GEORGE WASHINGTON
CHAIM WEIZMANN
WOODROW WILSON
XERXES
EMILIANO ZAPATA
ZHOU ENLAI

CHELSEA HOUSE PUBLISHERS

ON LEADERSHIP

Arthur M. Schlesinger, jr.

LEADERSHIP, it may be said, is really what makes the world go round. Love no doubt smooths the passage; but love is a private transaction between consenting adults. Leadership is a public transaction with history. The idea of leadership affirms the capacity of individuals to move, inspire, and mobilize masses of people so that they act together in pursuit of an end. Sometimes leadership serves good purposes, sometimes bad; but whether the end is benign or evil, great leaders are those men and women who leave their personal stamp on history.

Now, the very concept of leadership implies the proposition that individuals can make a difference. This proposition has never been universally accepted. From classical times to the present day, eminent thinkers have regarded individuals as no more than the agents and pawns of larger forces, whether the gods and goddesses of the ancient world or, in the modern era, race, class, nation, the dialectic, the will of the people, the spirit of the times, history itself. Against such forces, the individual dwindles into insignificance.

So contends the thesis of historical determinism. Tolstoy's great novel *War and Peace* offers a famous statement of the case. Why, Tolstoy asked, did millions of men in the Napoleonic Wars, denying their human feelings and their common sense, move back and forth across Europe slaughtering their fellows? "The war," Tolstoy answered, "was bound to happen simply because it was bound to happen." All prior history predetermined it. As for leaders, they, Tolstoy said, "are but the labels that serve to give a name to an end and, like labels, they have the least possible connection with the event." The greater the leader, "the more conspicuous the inevitability and the predestination of every act he commits." The leader, said Tolstoy, is "the slave of history."

Determinism takes many forms. Marxism is the determinism of class. Nazism the determinism of race. But the idea of men and women as the slaves of history runs athwart the deepest human instincts. Rigid determinism abolishes the idea of human freedom—

the assumption of free choice that underlies every move we make, every word we speak, every thought we think. It abolishes the idea of human responsibility, since it is manifestly unfair to reward or punish people for actions that are by definition beyond their control. No one can live consistently by any deterministic creed. The Marxist states prove this themselves by their extreme susceptibility to the cult of leadership.

More than that, history refutes the idea that individuals make no difference. In December 1931 a British politician crossing Park Avenue in New York City between 76th and 77th Streets around 10:30 P.M. looked in the wrong direction and was knocked down by an automobile—a moment, he later recalled, of a man aghast, a world aglare: "I do not understand why I was not broken like an eggshell or squashed like a gooseberry." Fourteen months later an American politician, sitting in an open car in Miami, Florida, was fired on by an assassin; the man beside him was hit. Those who believe that individuals make no difference to history might well ponder whether the next two decades would have been the same had Mario Constasino's car killed Winston Churchill in 1931 and Giuseppe Zangara's bullet killed Franklin Roosevelt in 1933. Suppose, in addition, that Adolf Hitler had been killed in the street fighting during the Munich *Putsch* of 1923 and that Lenin had died of typhus during World War I. What would the 20th century be like now?

For better or for worse, individuals do make a difference. "The notion that a people can run itself and its affairs anonymously," wrote the philosopher William James, "is now well known to be the silliest of absurdities. Mankind does nothing save through initiatives on the part of inventors, great or small, and imitation by the rest of us—these are the sole factors in human progress. Individuals of genius show the way, and set the patterns, which common people then adopt and follow."

Leadership, James suggests, means leadership in thought as well as in action. In the long run, leaders in thought may well make the greater difference to the world. But, as Woodrow Wilson once said, "Those only are leaders of men, in the general eye, who lead in action. . . . It is at their hands that new thought gets its translation into the crude language of deeds." Leaders in thought often invent in solitude and obscurity, leaving to later generations the tasks of imitation. Leaders in action—the leaders portrayed in this series—have to be effective in their own time.

And they cannot be effective by themselves. They must act in response to the rhythms of their age. Their genius must be adapted, in a phrase of William James's, "to the receptivities of the moment." Leaders are useless without followers. "There goes the mob," said the French politician hearing a clamor in the streets. "I am their leader. I must follow them." Great leaders turn the inchoate emotions of the mob to purposes of their own. They seize on the opportunities of their time, the hopes, fears, frustrations, crises, potentialities. They succeed when events have prepared the way for them, when the community is awaiting to be aroused, when they can provide the clarifying and organizing ideas. Leadership ignites the circuit between the individual and the mass and thereby alters history.

It may alter history for better or for worse. Leaders have been responsible for the most extravagant follies and most monstrous crimes that have beset suffering humanity. They have also been vital in such gains as humanity has made in individual freedom, religious and racial tolerance, social justice, and respect for human rights.

There is no sure way to tell in advance who is going to lead for good and who for evil. But a glance at the gallery of men and women in *World Leaders—Past and Present* suggests some useful tests.

One test is this: Do leaders lead by force or by persuasion? By command or by consent? Through most of history leadership was exercised by the divine right of authority. The duty of followers was to defer and to obey. "Theirs not to reason why / Theirs but to do and die." On occasion, as with the so-called enlightened despots of the 18th century in Europe, absolutist leadership was animated by humane purposes. More often, absolutism nourished the passion for domination, land, gold, and conquest and resulted in tyranny.

The great revolution of modern times has been the revolution of equality. The idea that all people should be equal in their legal condition has undermined the old structure of authority, hierarchy, and deference. The revolution of equality has had two contrary effects on the nature of leadership. For equality, as Alexis de Tocqueville pointed out in his great study *Democracy in America*, might mean equality in servitude as well as equality in freedom.

"I know of only two methods of establishing equality in the political world," Tocqueville wrote. "Rights must be given to every citizen, or none at all to anyone . . . save one, who is the master of all." There was no middle ground "between the sovereignty of all and the absolute power of one man." In his astonishing prediction of 20th-century totalitarian dictatorship, Tocqueville explained how the revolution of equality could lead to the *"Führerprinzip"* and more terrible absolutism than the world had ever known.

But when rights are given to every citizen and the sovereignty of all is established, the problem of leadership takes a new form, becomes more exacting than ever before. It is easy to issue commands and enforce them by the rope and the stake, the concentration camp and the *gulag.* It is much harder to use argument and achievement to overcome opposition and win consent. The Founding Fathers of the United States understood the difficulty. They believed that history had given them the opportunity to decide, as Alexander Hamilton wrote in the first Federalist Paper, whether men are indeed capable of basing government on "reflection and choice, or whether they are forever destined to depend . . . on accident and force."

Government by reflection and choice called for a new style of leadership and a new quality of followership. It required leaders to be responsive to popular concerns, and it required followers to be active and informed participants in the process. Democracy does not eliminate emotion from politics; sometimes it fosters demagoguery; but it is confident that, as the greatest of democratic leaders put it, you cannot fool all of the people all of the time. It measures leadership by results and retires those who overreach or falter or fail.

It is true that in the long run despots are measured by results too. But they can postpone the day of judgment, sometimes indefinitely, and in the meantime they can do infinite harm. It is also true that democracy is no guarantee of virtue and intelligence in government, for the voice of the people is not necessarily the voice of God. But democracy, by assuring the right of opposition, offers built-in resistance to the evils inherent in absolutism. As the theologian Reinhold Niebuhr summed it up, "Man's capacity for justice makes democracy possible, but man's inclination to injustice makes democracy necessary."

A second test for leadership is the end for which power is sought. When leaders have as their goal the supremacy of a master race or the promotion of totalitarian revolution or the acquisition and exploitation of colonies or the protection of greed and privilege or the preservation of personal power, it is likely that their leadership will do little to advance the cause of humanity. When their goal is the abolition of slavery, the liberation of women, the enlargement of opportunity for the poor and powerless, the extension of equal rights to racial minorities, the defense of the freedoms of expression and opposition, it is likely that their leadership will increase the sum of human liberty and welfare.

Leaders have done great harm to the world. They have also conferred great benefits. You will find both sorts in this series. Even "good" leaders must be regarded with a certain wariness. Leaders are not demigods; they put on their trousers one leg after another just like ordinary mortals. No leader is infallible, and every leader needs to be reminded of this at regular intervals. Irreverence irritates leaders but is their salvation. Unquestioning submission corrupts leaders and demeans followers. Making a cult of a leader is always a mistake. Fortunately hero worship generates its own antidote. "Every hero," said Emerson, "becomes a bore at last."

The signal benefit the great leaders confer is to embolden the rest of us to live according to our own best selves, to be active, insistent, and resolute in affirming our own sense of things. For great leaders attest to the reality of human freedom against the supposed inevitabilities of history. And they attest to the wisdom and power that may lie within the most unlikely of us, which is why Abraham Lincoln remains the supreme example of great leadership. A great leader, said Emerson, exhibits new possibilities to all humanity. "We feed on genius. . . . Great men exist that there may be greater men."

Great leaders, in short, justify themselves by emancipating and empowering their followers. So humanity struggles to master its destiny, remembering with Alexis de Tocqueville: "It is true that around every man a fatal circle is traced beyond which he cannot pass; but within the wide verge of that circle he is powerful and free; as it is with man, so with communities."

1

The Gray General

Early in the afternoon of April 9, 1865, three horsemen entered the yard of a red-brick mansion in the village of Appomattox Courthouse, Virginia. In front, dressed in the gray uniform of the Confederate States army, rode Sergeant G. W. Tucker. Behind Tucker came Colonel Orville Babcock, with two stars sewn to the shoulder of his dark blue uniform, identifying him as an officer of the United States. Alongside Babcock, mounted on a magnificent gray charger, rode a man dressed in an immaculate gray uniform with a scarlet sash at the waist. He was General Robert E. Lee, commander of the Confederate Army of Northern Virginia. As he entered the broad, tree-shaded yard, dismounted, and turned his horse over to Sergeant Tucker, Lee wore a sad and weary expression on his sun-bronzed face. He had come to this house to offer the surrender of his army and to help bring about an end to the war between the states that had raged across America for the last four years.

I did only what my duty demanded. I could have taken no other course without dishonor. And if it all were to be done over again, I should act in precisely the same manner.
—ROBERT E. LEE

Although Robert E. Lee abhorred slavery and was not a secessionist, his loyalties were with his home state of Virginia and the South during the American Civil War. He became a military adviser to Confederate president Jefferson Davis, who later appointed him commander of all the Southern armies.

General Lee and his stunning gray charger, Traveller, frequently visited the battlefields to bolster the resolve of the Confederate troops during the American Civil War. Although the Union forces greatly outnumbered Lee's battalions, his troops made up for what they lacked in manpower with courage and determination.

Lee did not have much choice. The exhausted Army of Northern Virginia, once the most feared body of troops in North America, lay stretched out along four miles of road just outside Appomattox Courthouse. Lee's gaunt soldiers wore tattered, bloodstained uniforms, and many of them had no shoes. Although some 25,000 men were gathered along the line of march, barely 8,000 could shoulder a musket and fight. The rest consisted of men pushed past the limits of endurance who struggled valiantly just to keep moving. Few of the Confederates had eaten a decent meal since April 7; Lee had spent the last two days desperately maneuvering away from his Federal pursuers in an effort to reach Appomattox Station, where provisions had been sent by the Confederate government. Despite their hunger and the overwhelming superiority in numbers and equipment of their opponents, Lee's men burned to continue fighting. They considered their general and the cause of Confederate independence to be one and the same; to them the white-bearded Virginian, in the words of his son Robert E. Lee, Jr., "represented cause, country, and all."

Lee had hoped, after reaching Appomattox Station, to feed his men and head south to join up with the army of General Joseph E. Johnston in North Carolina. United, the two generals could have mounted the semblance of a worthy resistance against the massive Union forces arrayed against them. This day, however, Lee had to face the final hopelessness of his army's struggle for survival. Well-equipped and well-fed Union forces, led by Lieutenant General Ulysses S. Grant, pressed hard upon the rear guard and flanks of Lee's rapidly dissolving host. Grant had also managed to place a strong force of infantry squarely across Lee's path, blocking the last remaining hope Lee had of reaching the supplies his starving men so desperately needed. Lee could only surrender or face total destruction.

The country for which Lee fought seemed hardly in better shape than his army. Union forces had captured Wilmington, North Carolina, the last open port in the Southern states, leaving the Confederacy completely isolated from the outside world. Federal cavalry swept through Alabama, capturing at Selma the South's only surviving war matériel manufacturing center. Lee's own desperate bid for survival

On April 5, 1865, Union troops swept through Alabama, capturing the naval foundry at Selma, the South's last surviving war munitions manufacturing center. The taking of the Selma foundry dashed whatever hope remained for a Southern victory.

had left the capital city of the Confederate states, Richmond, Virginia, unprotected. The resulting threat of capture had forced Confederate president Jefferson Davis and the rest of the Confederate government to flee to Danville, near the North Carolina border. As Lee mounted the steps leading up to the mansion's pillared front porch, he knew that the final defeat of the Army of Northern Virginia meant the ultimate collapse of the cause for which it had fought.

Lee and Babcock walked across the broad porch and entered the house. The residence belonged to Major Wilmer McLean, who ironically had moved to Appomattox Courthouse in the hope of avoiding the war completely. The comfortable furnishings and paintings on the wall gave witness to McLean's position as an upper middle class Virginian farmer. Lee's military secretary, Colonel Charles Marshall, met the two men inside and showed them into McLean's parlor. The slender, sandy-haired Marshall wore thick wire-rimmed glasses that combined with a thin mustache and light goatee to give him a perpetually thoughtful expression. Despite his best efforts to improve his appearance by borrowing a fresh shirt collar and a dress sword, Marshall's gray uniform betrayed the wear and tear of the last few days' march.

Lee sat down in a chair next to a marble-topped table where he could look out of a window southward, across the broad valley of the Appomattox River, to where his battered army lay resting. The three men chatted pleasantly for a while, until the sudden clatter of horse hooves outside announced the arrival of a large body of mounted men. Lee rose and stood impassively as Colonel Babcock strode forward and opened the door. A dark-haired, bearded man of middle height, wearing a dark blue, mud-spattered Federal private's uniform, entered the parlor, took stock of its occupants, and crossed over to Lee. Despite the newcomer's lack of ostentation, Lee knew instantly that he faced Ulysses Grant, general in chief of the Union armies.

Grant took off his gloves, extended his hand, and said quietly, "General Lee." Lee accepted the outstretched hand and returned the greeting. The Federal commander turned and called in five of his officers before taking a seat in an old office chair near the center of the parlor. The tension was palpable. Grant introduced the Confederate commander to his subordinates. As Lee shook hands with Colonel Ely Parker, an American Indian, he stared hard at him for a moment before saying, "I am glad to see one real American here." Parker replied, "We are all Americans."

After the introductions, Grant politely tried to break the tension: "I met you once before, General Lee, while we were serving in Mexico, when you came from General Scott's headquarters to visit Garland's brigade, to which I then belonged. I have always remembered your appearance, and I think I should have recognized you anywhere." Lee replied somewhat stiffly, "Yes, I know I met you on that occasion, and I have often thought of it and tried to recollect how you looked, but I have never been able to recall a single feature." Unruffled, Grant began to enthusiastically pursue common memories of the Mexican War, prompting Lee after a while to bring him back to the topic at hand: "I suppose, General Grant, that the object of our present meeting is fully understood. I asked to see you to ascertain upon what terms you would receive the surrender of my army."

Although he had the Army of Northern Virginia in a position such that he could demand unconditional surrender, Grant had no intention of humiliating Lee or of forcing the proud Confederate army to fight to the finish for honor's sake. He hoped instead to create an atmosphere of reconciliation between the two halves of a divided nation. Grant briefly outlined what he had in mind: All Confederate officers and men were to return to their homes under a promise not to take up arms against the U.S. government, unless officially exchanged for Federal prisoners held by the Confederacy. He further asked that all equipment belonging to the Army of Northern Virginia be delivered up as captured property. With a nod that masked his deep relief at the leniency of the terms, Lee gave his assent.

Colonel Ely Parker. When Lee met with Ulysses S. Grant at Appomattox Courthouse to offer his surrender, the Confederate general shook the hand of Parker, an American Indian, who was also present and said, "I am glad to see one real American here." Parker responded, "We are all Americans."

General Lee's surrender to General Grant at Appomattox Courthouse took place on April 9, 1865. Although Jefferson Davis — and scattered pockets of Southern resistance — continued the struggle for another month, Lee's surrender at Appomattox, in effect, marked the end of the Civil War.

Grant then began to talk about the possibilities of a general peace. He hoped to use Lee's influence to bring about a surrender on the part of the Confederacy as a whole. Lee, who had no intention of entering into negotiations that he considered to be the right of the Confederate government, merely nodded politely. Anxious not to have the painful ordeal of his personal surrender prolonged, Lee finally said, "I presume, General Grant, we have both carefully considered the proper steps to be taken, and I would suggest that you commit to writing the terms you have proposed, so that they may be formally acted upon."

Grant agreed and called for his order book. Colonel Parker brought out a small table for the general in chief, who lit a pipe, puffed furiously for a moment, and then began writing. After a short while he rose to hand the book to Lee and asked him to read it over. Lee pushed aside a few books on the table next to him, carefully wiped his spectacles with his handkerchief, set them slowly on his nose, and began to read. He discovered a missing word; after confirming this with Grant, he felt around in vain

for a pencil. Colonel Parker stepped forward and handed him one. Lee made the correction, then absentmindedly twirled the pencil in his fingers as he studied the last part of the document. His face noticeably brightened as he read that Grant proposed to allow Confederate officers to keep their personal sidearms and horses. He looked up and said, "This will have a very happy effect on my army."

Grant replied that if Lee found the terms acceptable as written, he would have them copied out for signature. Lee hesitated. The cavalry and artillerymen of the Army of Northern Virginia had brought their own personal horses to war. Small farmers for the most part, the men had little hope of bringing in a crop for their families without their animals. Lee asked that the enlisted men of his army who claimed a horse or a mule be allowed to take the animal home with them. Grant replied, "You will find that the terms as written do not allow this." Lee glanced over the document again and said, "No, I see the terms do not allow it; that is clear." His face, however, betrayed his disappointment. Grant, swiftly comprehending Lee's distress, offered to grant the Confederate general's wish in separate orders. A grateful Lee replied, "This will have the best possible effect upon the men. It will be very gratifying, and will do much toward conciliating our people."

Grant gave his order book to Colonel Parker for copying, and Lee asked Colonel Marshall to draft a reply. As the two secretaries bent to their tasks, Colonel Babcock whispered to Grant, left the room, and returned with 12 more Union officers, who arranged themselves behind their commander with the sound of clanking spurs. Lee rose, went over to the group, and greeted each of the newcomers as Grant introduced them. He then turned to Grant and outlined one remaining difficulty. Some 1,500 Union prisoners languished inside the Confederate lines, suffering from the same lack of food as their captors. Would Grant consider forwarding to the Army of Northern Virginia the supplies Lee had expected to meet at Appomattox Station? The gathered Federal officers stirred uncomfortably and glanced over at one of their number, General Philip Sheridan, who the previous night had captured those very provisions. Grant, to avoid confronting Lee with yet another humiliation, proposed sending 25,000 rations immediately to the starving Confederates. Lee accepted with obvious relief.

The white-haired Virginian returned to his seat and studied the letter that Colonel Marshall had written. After making a few corrections, he had Marshall rewrite it. In its final form, the letter read:

> Headquarters, Army of Northern Virginia
> April 9, 1865
> Lieut. Gen. U. S. Grant,
> Commanding Armies of the United States.
> General:
> I have received your letter of this date containing the terms of surrender of the Army of Northern Virginia as proposed by you. As they are substantially the same as those expressed in your letter of [April 8], they are accepted. I will proceed to designate the proper officers to carry the stipulations into effect. Very respectfully, your obedient servant,
> R. E. Lee

At 3:45 P.M., Lee signed the letter. As he did so, Grant searched his former opponent's face, trying to determine whether or not he welcomed the end of the fighting. The Union commander could not, however, glean any hint of Lee's emotions.

With the capitulation officially accomplished, the gathered officers conversed pleasantly. Grant apologized to Lee for his slovenly dress, explaining that Lee's request for a conference had caught him four miles away from his luggage. Lee in turn expressed gratitude that Grant had not delayed for the sake of appearances. At about 4:00 P.M. he picked up his hat and gloves, shook hands with General Grant, bowed courteously to the assembled officers, and left the parlor. A group of Federals waiting on the porch for news of the proceedings jumped to their feet and saluted as the Confederate commander crossed to the stairs. Lee, his face mirroring his sorrow and fatigue, responded politely. At the top of the steps he stopped, drew on his gloves, and struck his left fist in the palm of his right hand several times. Not seeing his horse, he called out in a husky, strained voice, "Orderly! Orderly!" Sergeant Tucker responded from around the left corner of the house, where the big gray horse browsed hungrily on the lawn. Lee walked over to his mount. As Sergeant Tucker arranged the bridle, Lee reached up and tenderly smoothed out the horse's forelock. Then, with an audible sigh, he slowly raised himself into the saddle and began to move across the lawn, followed by Colonel Marshall. At that moment, Grant came hurriedly down the steps with his head down and walked toward his own horse. When he spotted Lee crossing his path, he stopped and raised his hat. The Federal soldiers gathered on the porch and in the yard also removed their hats in a silent echo of Grant's salute. Lee raised his own in return. Without a word, he then turned and urged his horse out into the gathering evening to give his men the bitter news that their long, gallant fight had ended.

2

Training for War

In the early summer of 1810, young Robert Edward Lee experienced his first great loss. As his sister Ann led him by the hand out of the front door of Stratford Hall, the three-year-old boy saw his older brothers, Carter and Smith, and his pregnant mother, Ann Carter Lee, waiting with a carriage in the driveway of the Lees' ancestral home. Behind the carriage stood a cart piled high with trunks, books, Robert's cradle, and the family's four black slaves. Stratford, on the south bank of the Potomac River near the broad waters of Chesapeake Bay, reflected in its weed-choked gardens and bare, abandoned atmosphere the hard times that had befallen the Lees of Virginia. Robert's father, the legendary Henry "Light-Horse Harry" Lee, hero of the American Revolution and favorite of General George Washington, had not revealed as much talent for civilian life as he had for the military. Despite a sparkling political career in the Virginia and federal legislatures, three terms as governor of Virginia, and Washington's

Her affections were trampled on by a heartless and depraved profligate, I am right as to time. One fortnight was her dream of happiness from which she awoke to a lifetime of misery.
—Anonymous relative of Ann Carter Lee's, on her marriage to Henry Lee

Robert E. Lee, the son of the American revolutionary war hero Henry "Light-Horse Harry" Lee, entered the U.S. Military Academy at West Point, New York — historically the educational training ground for America's greatest military leaders — in 1825.

As a civilian, Henry Lee was often harassed for his political views and constantly pursued by his creditors. After he was badly beaten by a mob outraged by his opposition to the War of 1812, he fled to Barbados, leaving his children in the care of his wife, Ann.

steady support, Light-Horse Harry could not keep his weakness for financial speculation from scattering both his own fortune and that of his young second wife to the four winds. At the moment, he languished in debtor's prison. His first wife, Matilda, had recognized her husband's weakness and had put Stratford out of his reach by placing the estate in trust for her eldest son before she died. That son, Henry Lee, had now come of age, forcing Ann and her four children to find another home.

Ann Lee had resolved to move her family to Alexandria, just across the Potomac from the new federal capital at Washington, D.C. The Lees had many relatives in the area, and the town boasted many veterans who fondly remembered serving under the dashing Light-Horse Harry. Two years after their arrival, Light-Horse Harry fell victim to an angry mob outraged by his firm opposition to the War of 1812. Cruelly disfigured, broken in spirit, and still pursued relentlessly by creditors, he fled to the island of Barbados to recover. Left on her own to raise the children, Ann resolved not to let them repeat her husband's mistakes. She insisted that they learn strict self-control, financial discipline, and a firm sense of honor. Young Robert listened and learned, with the result that those elements became strong parts of his character. When his education progressed beyond the limits of her tutoring, Ann sent Robert to a local private school maintained by her family.

The death of Light-Horse Harry in 1818 at last brought relief from creditors. However, Ann became increasingly ill, most probably from tuberculosis. By 1820 she needed regular nursing. Of her boys, only the 13-year-old Robert remained at home to care for his mother. The young boy smoothly stepped into adult shoes, managing the servants, maintaining the stables, and standing in constant attendance at his mother's bedside. Despite his new responsibilities, however, Robert managed to find time to become an accomplished skater and dancer and to ride on the hunt in the rolling hills behind the town.

In 1823 he finished his schooling, and the question of how he should spend his life became pressing. He did not stand to inherit enough money or property to settle down as a landed gentleman. His eldest brother, Charles, had gone to Harvard and now had a promising career as a lawyer in Washington. Robert, however, had little interest in law. The thought of medicine or the ministry similarly failed to arouse any enthusiasm. His other brother, Smith, had received a midshipman's berth in the navy; perhaps the youngest Lee son could join the army. Once Robert reached his decision, his extended family mobilized all of its resources to obtain for him one of the rare and coveted appointments as a West Point cadet. He received a letter of recommendation signed by five U.S. senators and three members of the House of Representatives. His half brother Henry sent a letter to the secretary of war,

Ann Lee, a strong-willed woman who believed in the virtues of self-discipline and honor, instilled these values in her children. Her son Robert, a potent example of his mother's sound influence, was throughout his life first and foremost a gentleman, even amid the chaos and desperation of war.

Artillery practice at West Point. Lee, an outstanding student at the U.S. Military Academy, was named staff sergeant of cadets after his first year and soon thereafter was appointed acting professor of mathematics. He graduated second in his class in 1829.

John C. Calhoun, invoking the memory of Light-Horse Harry's many services to his country in the Revolution. Robert traveled in person to meet Secretary Calhoun and Senator Andrew Jackson from Tennessee. The combination of family support and Robert's own courtly and intelligent manner resulted in orders to report to West Point with the class entering in 1825.

In June of that year, the 18-year-old Lee, with his regulation army leather trunk, traveled by steamer and stagecoach to West Point, New York. Although it had been established on its bluff overlooking the Hudson River 23 years earlier, the appearance of the U.S. Military Academy had none of the grandeur suggested by its name. Dormitories, a mess hall, and a schoolhouse, all covered with stucco to give the required military uniformity, surrounded a wide drill field and parade ground. The rules and regu-

lations matched the utilitarian severity of the buildings. Dormitory rooms and personal appearance had to be immaculate. Cadets could not cook or eat in their rooms, and no alcohol, tobacco, playing cards, or novels were permitted. A violation of these or any of the myriad other regulations resulted in one or more demerits. Enough demerits could seriously affect a cadet's status upon graduation. In September, the school year officially opened, and Lee began classes in mathematics and French, in addition to ceaseless drills out on the parade ground. One of the few breaks in the routine came when he witnessed the court-martial of Cadet Jefferson Davis for leaving the grounds and drinking alcohol. At the end of the first year, Lee emerged third in his class, with no demerits to his name. He promptly received the honor of promotion to the rank of staff sergeant of cadets.

As the years passed, Lee learned to drill with a musket and to maneuver and fire artillery pieces. His mathematical skills progressed rapidly, and eventually he was appointed acting assistant professor of mathematics. The handsome Virginian also made a lasting impression on his fellow students. Some found his good looks and dignified manner intimidating, whereas others admired him. One wrote, "His personal appearance surpassed in manly beauty that of any cadet in the corps. Though firm in his position and perfectly erect, he had none of the stiffness so often assumed by men who affect to be very strict in their ideas of what is military." Lee's continued presence near the top of his class seemed to ensure his eventual eligibility for the U.S. Army's elite branch, the Army Engineering Corps, the goal of nearly all ambitious cadets.

The high standards, grueling routine, and strict discipline at the academy proved too demanding for many cadets. As the final examinations for the class of 1829 approached, only two of the four Virginians who had entered in 1825 remained. Conscious of their responsibility as the sole representatives of their native state, Lee and his fellow survivor, Joseph E. Johnston, drew together and developed a lasting friendship. At the beginning of June 1829 a board of examiners convened for a two-week period of oral testing, which the cadets referred to as the Inquisition. When the dust settled, Lee had emerged first in artillery and tactics and second overall in his class. His success placed him in a position to choose his branch of the service. He quickly chose a commission as lieutenant of engineers.

In the summer of 1829, Lee returned to Virginia to find his mother at the estate of family friends, near death from her illness. Lee immediately assumed his old role as nurse but could only watch helplessly on July 10 as Ann Lee died.

With his mother gone, Lee found his thoughts continually wandering to the massive Greek revival mansion of Arlington, on the southern bank of the Potomac overlooking Washington, D.C. The estate belonged to George Washington Parke Custis, Martha Washington's grandson and George Washington's adopted son. Lee had met Custis's only daughter, Mary, while on furlough from West Point. The plain, aristocratic-featured young blonde, whose outspokenness and slightly self-righteous religious fervor made her less than attractive for most potential suitors, fascinated the young lieutenant. In August, Lee asked the young heiress to marry him. Custis did not like the idea of his daughter marrying a son of the irresponsible Light-Horse Harry Lee. Mary's mother had to convince her husband to accept the match.

Lee spent the next five years on fort-building duty in Georgia and eastern Virginia, pausing only in the summer of 1831 for his wedding. He threw himself into his work, gaining a firsthand look at the problems of practical military engineering. He applied the principles of economy that his mother had taught him to his work and quickly developed a reputation for bringing engineering projects in on time and on budget. Lee also displayed political skills that soon became characteristic: an ability to combine initiative with tact and deference in dealing with his superiors and a fine touch for making the men under him work willingly and cheerfully. Despite his success, however, Lee found his work uninspiring. When he received the chance in October 1834 to transfer to the Engineering Corps Office in Washington, Lee accepted in the hopes of finding something more challenging to do.

Washington, D.C., in 1834 displayed a strange combination of the majesty of the young Federal Union with the backwardness of a struggling new village. Mud streets and board sidewalks coexisted with fine government buildings and lavish homes. Barnyard animals grazed freely on the lawn of the unfinished Capitol. Despite its lack of refinement, however, the city's social life hummed whenever Congress was in session. Lee found himself frustrated by the routines of bureaucratic work and found escape making the rounds of Washington society. He placed Mary and their new baby with her parents at Arlington and spent his free hours at parties and receptions, delighting in the assortment

Lee met Mary Custis, the daughter of George Washington's adopted son, George Washington Parke Custis, while he was on furlough from West Point. They were married in June 1831.

of beautiful and well-bred young women that Washington had to offer. Although he loved his wife and remained faithful to her, the handsome young lieutenant could seldom resist the temptation to flirt when opportunity presented itself.

Despite a brief reprieve from boredom helping to survey the border between Ohio and Michigan, Lee lapsed into a depression that Mary's illness after the birth of their second child did nothing to help. He even briefly considered leaving the army to try to find more fulfilling work in private engineering. In April 1836, Lee volunteered to help direct a project to keep the ever-changing Mississippi River from silting up the harbor at St. Louis, Missouri. Although funding cuts halted the project in the fall of 1840, Lee managed to reopen a channel to the city for shipping, winning a promotion to captain of engineers in the process.

The lack of enthusiasm for military appropriations in Congress that halted the St. Louis project left Lee little to look forward to other than a brief tour of inspection of the coastal defenses in the Carolinas. He ended up in New York City with an assignment to improve the harbor fortifications, and his old sense of futility and frustration returned. The only lightening of the gloom came in 1844 with an assignment to sit on the examining board for the Inquisition at West Point. Also on the board was the general in chief of the army, Major General Winfield Scott. The strict Scott, nicknamed Old Fuss and Feathers in the ranks, noticed Lee's intelligence and good judgment during the two weeks of the examinations and left West Point with a deep impression of Lee's qualities that later stood the young Virginian in good stead. For the time being, however, Lee could only return to New York City's Fort Hamilton and contemplate a future that seemed to hold nothing more in store for him than endless fort repair.

The Mexican War soon put an end to Lee's frustration. On March 1, 1845, outgoing president John Tyler, responding to public pressure, signed a treaty with the newly independent state of Texas, incor-

It is true we bullied her. Of that I am ashamed, as She was the weaker party, But we have since by way of Set-off drubbed her handsomely, & in a manner that women might be ashamed of. It would be curious now if we Should refuse to accept the territory we have forced her to relinquish. . . . It would be marvellously like us.

—ROBERT E. LEE
on the Mexican War and its
aftermath

porating it into the Union. The Mexican government, despite having lost a war with Texas, still regarded the renegade territory as its property and broke off diplomatic relations with Washington. To further complicate the issue, the Texans claimed the Rio Grande as their southern border; the Mexicans maintained that Texas ended at the Nueces, 130 miles to the north. In January 1846, after negotiations failed, the new president, James Polk, ordered General Zachary Taylor and his men to occupy the area between the Nueces and the Rio Grande. Mexican efforts to dislodge Taylor and his troops led to several pitched battles in which American soldiers died. President Polk, taking advantage of public outrage, persuaded Congress on May 13 to declare war.

The Rio Grande, near El Paso, Texas. In 1845, U.S. president John Tyler signed a treaty that incorporated Texas into the Union, outraging the Mexican government, which claimed that the territory rightly belonged to Mexico. The United States and Mexico went to war to resolve the dispute.

General Zachary Taylor, or Old Rough and Ready, fought with distinction in the War of 1812 and later in the Mexican War. A brilliant military strategist, he badly defeated the Mexicans at Palo Alto, Resaca de la Palma, Monterrey, and Buena Vista. Taylor later became the 12th president of the United States.

Lee, observing events from his post at Fort Hamilton, felt that his government had behaved badly. He wrote to his wife, who was recovering at Arlington from the birth of their seventh child, "I never could see the advantage to be gained by sending General Taylor . . . unless it was to *invite* the Mexicans to attack [Taylor] on account of the feebleness of his force and thus bring on the war we had not the frankness or manliness at once to declare." Despite his distaste for the president's methods, Lee yearned to get out of New York and into the action. Instructions to prepare Fort Hamilton against possible attack by British forces intervening on the side of Mexico did little to help Lee's impatience. Finally, in August 1846, Lee received orders to report for duty to the army of Brigadier General John Wool in Texas.

On September 21, Lee rode into the town of San Antonio de Bexar, where General Wool's army prepared for its advance to the Rio Grande. The force at San Antonio formed part of a two-pronged attack on northern Mexico. General Taylor's forces headed for Monterrey; General Wool, operating under Taylor's command, had orders to cross the Rio Grande farther west and invade the Mexican state of Chihuahua. The high command hoped that these attacks, coupled with a tight naval blockade and simultaneous assaults on the Mexican territories of California and New Mexico, would quickly bring Mexico to her knees. On September 28, nearly 2,000 men left San Antonio and marched west. Topographical engineers fanned out ahead of the army, searching out the best routes for the small force to pass. Lee helped to direct the engineering teams that removed obstacles, improved roads, and built the necessary bridges. At the end of each day, Lee and his men laid out the army's camp for the night.

Monterrey, as it appeared in 1846, looking east from Independence Hill. The fortified city fell into American hands in one of the critical battles of the Mexican War as Zachary Taylor and some 10,000 cavalrymen advanced into Mexico that year.

In mid-October, the force crossed the Rio Grande. After hearing that General Taylor had taken Monterrey and finding the route westward into Chihuahua empty of water and too rough for his wagons, Wool spent the next several months marching southward through the eastern Sierra Madre to join up with his superior. A junction with part of General Taylor's forces at Saltillo brought the size of the army to 6,000 men, the largest group of soldiers Lee had ever seen.

Shortly after Christmas, Wool grew impatient with his inability to locate the Mexican forces on his front with any degree of accuracy. Lee volunteered to serve as a scout and rode out through the American lines at night with only a young Mexican boy as a guide. After about 20 miles he spotted campfires on a nearby hilltop. His guide grew terrified of capture and disappeared, leaving Lee to press on alone in strange country. He quickly determined that he faced not an enemy army but the camp of some Mexican shepherds. After questioning them in his halting Spanish and learning that the Mexican army lay some distance away, Lee returned and reported to General Wool. Instead of resting on his laurels, however, Lee slept for three hours and rode out into the mountains again with a cavalry escort. He returned with definite news of the enemy's position, prompting General Wool to promote Lee to acting inspector general of his army.

In January 1847, Lee received orders to report to the Gulf Coast, where General Winfield Scott was preparing an expedition to assault the coastal fortress of Veracruz, approximately 500 miles south of the mouth of the Rio Grande. A delighted Lee discovered on arrival that his old friend Joe Johnston, who had chosen the artillery service on leaving West Point, had also been assigned to the operation. General Scott quickly included Lee on his staff. On February 15, 1847, Scott's flotilla set sail with 6,000 troops. Lee and Johnston shared a cabin on Scott's flagship, the *Massachusetts*. On March 5, the fleet came in sight of the fortress overlooking Veracruz and met up with the grim black warships on blockade duty. The next day, Scott and his staff boarded

Brigadier General John Ellis Wool. During the Mexican War, Lee served under Wool, who was so impressed with the young man's courage and ability, particularly as a scout, that he made him acting inspector general of his army.

a small steamer and sailed close inshore to scout out landing beaches for the army. Lee got his first taste of hostile action when guns in the Mexican fortress began shooting, surrounding the small ship with splashes of poorly aimed cannon fire.

Two days later Lee watched from the deck of the *Massachusetts* as blue-clad infantry, carrying their muskets over their heads, sprang out of their boats, waded ashore, and raised the American flag over a group of sand dunes behind the beach. With the landing accomplished, General Scott ordered artillery batteries set up as quickly as possible in the hopes of shelling the city into submission. Lee handled the placement of the batteries, masking his movements so skillfully that the besieged Mexicans had little warning of his intentions. After eight days of hard labor under a blistering hot sun, with Mexican mortar shells whining overhead, the American batteries opened fire. Lee, directing fire from a naval battery commanded by his brother Smith, watched with distress as the American shells arched high into the sky and then fell with a terrifying roar behind the fortress walls. He wrote later, "My [heart] bled for the inhabitants. The soldiers I did not care for, but the women and children [were] terrible to think of. . . ." On March 27, the city surrendered. In his victory dispatch to Washington, Scott included Lee among the officers he singled out for praise.

In mid-April 1847, Scott's army left Veracruz and headed west toward Mexico City. The weary troops had to march for miles on sand heated by the scorching sun. Lee wrote to Mary that no one "at their comfortable homes can realize the exertions,

In January 1847, Lee took part in the bombardment of Veracruz, a coastal fortress about 500 miles south of the mouth of the Rio Grande. The assault was led by General Winfield Scott, who relied heavily on Lee's prowess as an engineer and artillery officer.

pains, and hardships of an army in the field, under a scorching sun and in an enervating atmosphere. . . . The crack of the whip and prick of the spear stimulates the animals, and man's untiring ardour drives the whole." At a mountain pass named Cerro Gordo, the American troops ran into fortifications backed by a large Mexican army. The Mexican president and commander in chief, General Antonio López de Santa Anna, assumed that the apparently rugged mountains on either side of the pass left the Americans no choice but to assault his almost impregnable position. Lee proposed to General Scott that they try to bypass the position anyway, and get into the Mexican rear. After scouting out a route around the Mexican left, Lee led a small party up the mountains, ferrying cannon up the slopes with ropes and pulleys, which attacked the Mexican rear at the same time that General Scott

launched a frontal assault. The ensuing battle routed the Mexicans, who gave up some 3,000 prisoners to the Americans. Lee received a brevet promotion (an honorary advance in title) to major for, in the words of General Scott, his "coolness and gallantry."

The army halted for three months at the town of Puebla to wait out attempts to negotiate a peace. When Scott learned that the negotiations had failed and that Santa Anna had run off with bribe money given to him by the American government, he decided to cut his supply line to the American fleet at Veracruz and march boldly on Mexico City. The 10,000-strong army picked its way through passes in the mountains that sometimes rose as high as 11,000 feet. Three days out of Puebla, Lee crested a ridge and found Mexico City spread out before him. A great green valley dotted with lakes and small villages and the towering white mass of Popocatepetl volcano looming ahead formed a magnificent backdrop for the houses and churches of Mexico's capital city. General Santa Anna did his best, performing strategic miracles in his attempt to organize a defense of the city. The Mexican soldiers, resplendent in their uniforms of red, white, and green, fought bravely. In the end, however, superior equipment and training enabled the Americans to advance. Lee once more proved his skill as a scout and engineer by finding a route through a tortured lava bed that Santa Anna had counted on being impassable. On September 13, the Americans successfully stormed into Mexico City, assisted by the ingenuity of a young brigade supply officer named Ulysses Grant, who managed to get a small cannon up into a church steeple and scatter the Mexican defenders below him.

Lee received another brevet promotion to lieutenant colonel for his role in the capture of Mexico City. General Scott, well aware of the debt he owed to the major of engineers from Virginia, wrote in a report that Lee's work was "the greatest feat of physical and moral courage performed by any individual, in my knowledge, pending the campaign." He further went on to call Lee the "very best soldier in the field"

that he had ever seen. Lee completed his military education during his time spent on General Scott's staff, having seen Scott abandon his line of communications and learned the value of bold and unorthodox maneuvers in bringing victory to an outnumbered force. In addition, Lee learned to trust his own capacities. With newly discovered pride, he wrote to Mary, "There are few men more healthy or more able to bear exposure and fatigue, nor do I know any of my personal associates that have under gone as much of either during this campaign." He had successfully combined the example of his mentor, Winfield Scott, with his West Point training and native courage and intelligence to become a well-rounded, self-confident soldier.

A young brigade supply officer by the name of Ulysses S. Grant takes part in the capture of Mexico City on September 13, 1847. Grant, who cleverly took aim from a church steeple, well out of the reach of enemy fire, distinguished himself in the Mexican War.

3

The Storm Breaks

On June 26, 1848, Brevet Colonel Robert E. Lee dismounted in front of the Custis mansion at Arlington. He strode into the front hall, where his family waited, and promptly embraced a visiting child as his own Robert, Jr. The five-year-old Rob, standing nearby, was mortified. All of Lee's children had trouble reconciling this strange man with the fairy-tale warrior that they had known of through letters for the last two years. Their father did not have much time to renew his acquaintance with them. The War Department sent the hero of Cerro Gordo on an inspection tour of forts in New England and to the Gulf of Mexico before assigning him to fort-repair duty in Baltimore, Maryland. Increasingly infirm from arthritis and resenting having to plan her life around her husband's military career, Mary stayed with her parents at Arlington and did not join her husband until 1850.

We must not be enemies. Though passion may have strained, it must not break our bonds of affection. The mystic chords of memory, stretching from every battlefield and patriot grave, to every living heart and hearthstone, all over this broad land, will yet swell the chorus of the Union, when again touched, as surely as they will be, by the better angels of our nature.
—ABRAHAM LINCOLN

Like Grant, Lee fought bravely during the Mexican War. He was made a lieutenant colonel for his role in the siege of Mexico City and was called "the very best soldier in the field" by General Scott. Following the war, Lee became superintendent of the U.S. Military Academy.

James Earl Brown, or Jeb, Stuart was a classmate of Custis Lee's at West Point. An outstanding student at the academy, Stuart later proved a fearless cavalry leader.

Lee shared with the rest of the U.S. Army a difficulty in adjusting to the placid life of peacetime. His restlessness deepened so that in 1849 he even considered serving with a group of Cuban revolutionaries planning to overthrow the Spanish colonial government. Despite his frustration, however, Lee felt unable to leave the army, which had given him a sense of purpose and of belonging he had not found in civilian life.

In May 1852, the War Department ordered Lee to West Point as the academy's new superintendent. Lee had serious doubts about his qualifications for the job and had little liking for administration after his experience in the Engineering Corps office in Washington. The War Department, however, overrode his polite attempt to decline the post, and on September 1, 1852, Lee became the academy's ninth commander. As superintendent, Lee tightened the academy's budget, made changes in the curriculum, and improved the cadets' quarters and uniforms. He worried about students with poor records and spent a great deal of time trying to help them. On weekends he opened the doors of his residence to student visits and quickly became known for making nervous cadets feel comfortable and at ease. His son Custis, a cadet in the class of 1854, became one of his favorite guests, as did a broad-shouldered, red-haired cadet from Virginia named James Earl Brown, or Jeb, Stuart. Lee gained a reputation for impartiality by recommending his nephew Fitz Lee for a court-martial on drinking charges, and he applied West Point standards to his own children, to the point of making Rob stand by and watch as his father did a military inspection of his room. Worried parents and congressmen out to protect their constituents hampered Lee's attempts to raise academic standards until 1853, when a new Democratic administration brought in the former cadet Jefferson Davis as secretary of war. Davis put a stop to all political interference with the academy, and he and Lee soon developed a high degree of mutual trust. Davis did have concerns about Lee's qualities as superintendent. Years later he wrote, "When . . . I visited the Academy and was surprised to see so many gray hairs on [Lee's] head, he confessed that the cadets did exceedingly worry him, and then it was perceptible that his sympathy with young people was rather an impediment than a qualification for the superintendency."

The massacre of a cavalry troop by the Sioux Indians in 1854 gave Davis the excuse he needed to push the creation of two new cavalry regiments through Congress. He promptly offered to make Lee second in command of the Second Cavalry, with confirmation of his rank as lieutenant colonel. The 48-year-old Lee, who did not see many prospects for promotion as an engineer, believed the cavalry promised a healthy outdoor life and the possibility of recapturing the excitement of the Mexican War. He placed his family at Arlington and in April 1855 joined his regiment in Louisville, Kentucky.

Instead of the frontier action he had hoped for, however, Lee soon found himself condemned to a seemingly endless round of court-martial duty.

The Sioux Indians, a peaceable people but always ready to defend their territory against intruders, inflicted casualties on Southern cavalry troops in 1854. This prompted Jefferson Davis, with the help of Congress, to create two new regiments, one of which was placed under Lee's command.

Court-martials required hundreds of miles on horseback before arriving at some distant fort to sit for hours on a panel while lawyers argued back and forth. Lee quickly fell into depression. The location of his first court-martial assignments did nothing to help his state of mind: The War Department ordered Lee to serve on panels at Fort Leavenworth and Fort Riley, in the Kansas Territory, where for the first time Americans were reaching for guns in an effort to solve the problem of slavery.

The conflict centered around the issue of the extension of slavery into the new territories won by westward migration and by victory in the Mexican War. Everyone on both sides acknowledged that the individual states had the right to prohibit or allow slavery within their own borders with no interference from the federal government. Slave owners from the Southern states, however, maintained that Congress had no constitutional power to restrict the right to private property (ie., slaves) in the territories belonging to the United States but not yet formally admitted to the Union. Northern abolitionists, firmly convinced of the moral evil of slavery, insisted that the federal government did have this right and that it should exercise it so as to leave slavery isolated in the states of the Deep South.

The conflict came to a head in the Kansas Territory in the mid-1850s. Northern abolition societies helped antislave settlers move into the territory and gave them rifles to defend themselves. Southern politicians encouraged proslavery men from neighboring Missouri to terrorize the "free soilers." As violence and ballot stuffing escalated on both sides, the situation in Kansas soon began to resemble a civil war. Lee, for his part, had little admiration for slavery. Although he felt that black Africans had benefited by their having been liberated from what was generally perceived as the barbarism of the African continent, Lee strongly supported gradual emancipation. However, he disliked the radical abolitionists in the North who favored immediate, unconditional freedom for the slaves. He felt that such a move would devastate both the freed slaves and the Southern economy. As he rode through Kansas in the fall of 1855, the rumors of violent passion and armed clashes must have shaken him. The officers who assembled with Lee at Fort Riley all pledged their loyalty to the Union, but since many, like Lee, came from Southern states, a tense atmosphere hung over the proceedings.

In March 1856, Lee finally received orders to rejoin the Second Cavalry in Texas. He spent 16 months at Camp Cooper, near modern-day Abilene, directing the resettlement of a tribe of Comanche Indians and chasing those who refused to cooperate. In July 1857, the War Department ordered him to take over command of the regiment. He had not been at headquarters in San Antonio for more than a few months when word arrived that George Washington Parke Custis had died. Lee immediately applied for leave and rushed home, arriving at Arlington in late October. He found that Custis had left a massive debt and had allowed Arlington and his other estates to fall into near ruin. To make matters worse, arthritis had made Mary a near invalid; she was totally incapable of managing her family's affairs.

In 1856–57, Lee was stationed at Camp Cooper, where he directed the resettlement of a tribe of Comanche Indians. In defense of their property, their families, and their culture, the Comanche were perhaps the most fearless fighters of all the Plains Indians.

Following in his father's footsteps, Custis Lee attended the U.S. Military Academy at West Point. Although his father was head of the school while he was in attendance, the young Lee received no special treatment from his teachers. In fact, Lee himself was very strict with his son, as he was with all the cadets.

Lee now found himself faced with the choice he had hitherto managed to avoid. He wrote to his former commander in Texas, Albert Sidney Johnston, "I have at last to decide the question I have staved off for 20 years, whether I am to continue in the Army all my life, or leave it now." When Winfield Scott offered to make Lee his military secretary, the Virginian turned the post down. He hesitated, however, to give up completely on the life of honor and noble glory he had glimpsed in Mexico. A life spent caring for his invalid wife and dealing with the neglected Custis estates had no lasting appeal. By the autumn of 1858, Lee had had enough of Arlington. He began to pull strings to get his son Custis transferred to Washington. With Custis near enough to run the estate, Lee could allow himself to return to the army.

On October 17, 1859, Jeb Stuart, now a tall, dashing cavalry lieutenant, galloped up to Arlington with orders for Lee to report to Washington. When he arrived at the War Department Lee heard news of an attack on the federal arsenal at Harpers Ferry, on the south bank of the Potomac River in northeastern Virginia. The department ordered him to take two companies of marines to the town and find out what was going on. When Lee, Stuart, and the marines arrived at Harpers Ferry late that night, they found units of the Virginia militia and local farmers with squirrel guns surrounding the arsenal's fire-engine building. Inside, a group of armed men led by a white-bearded abolitionist named John Brown held a group of hostages and exchanged occasional shots with the crowd outside. John Brown had made his reputation in the slavery dispute in Kansas. Convinced that God had ordained him to free the slaves, the radical abolitionist led raids on proslavery settlers, including one gruesome massacre on the Pottawatomie River in 1856 that earned him the nickname of Pottawatomie John. The self-proclaimed saint had organized the raid on Harpers Ferry in the hopes of seizing federal weapons, freeing local slaves, and igniting an insurrection throughout Virginia, Tennessee, and the Carolinas. Lee placed his men around the building and ordered Jeb Stuart to go in at dawn and deliver a surrender demand. When the young cavalryman signaled that Brown had no intention of giving himself up, Lee ordered the marines to attack. Within minutes, the soldiers freed the hostages and captured the raiders.

A Virginia court condemned John Brown to death. Lee remained in command of troops at Harpers Ferry to prevent unrest during the hanging and to quiet the fears of Virginians afraid of further abolitionist raids. As the day of the hanging approached, shock waves from the raid raced out across the nation and shattered what remained of hopes for a compromise on the slavery issue. In the North, church bells tolled and flags flew at half-mast as orators loudly praised John Brown as a martyr to the cause of freedom. Southern politicians began to blame the North as a whole and the new free-soil Republican party in particular for the actions of a single zealot and passionately declared their intention to secede from the Union if a "black Republican" won the presidency in the upcoming 1860 elections. Lee personally had his doubts about an organized attempt by the North to interfere with slavery in Southern states. In his report on the raid he wrote, "The result proves that the plan was the attempt of a fanatic or madman." As the bitter controversy raged across the nation, Lee quietly returned to Arlington, handed the reins of the estate over to Custis, and set off to rejoin his regiment in Texas.

He wound up in San Antonio in temporary command of the entire Texas military department. Apart from a brief stint chasing a Mexican bandit, Lee settled into headquarters routine and soon felt the familiar sensations of depression and futility overtake him. National events, however, soon surpassed Lee's private concerns. At its convention in Charleston, South Carolina, in April 1860, the Democratic party split over the slavery issue. An attempt in June to reconvene the convention in Baltimore only led to the announcement of two separate Democratic candidates. Radicals in the Democratic party stoked the fires of division, hoping that a shattered party

I John Brown am now quite certain that the crimes of this guilty land; will never be purged away; but with blood.
—JOHN BROWN
in a note handed to one of his jailers before his execution

Abraham Lincoln was elected president of the United States in November 1860, amid increasing tension between the Northern and Southern states over the issue of slavery. Soon after Lincoln's inauguration, the Confederate army opened fire on Fort Sumter, and the Civil War began.

would lose to the Republican candidate Abraham Lincoln and give Southern states a reason to secede. Lee watched the campaign anxiously from San Antonio, hoping against hope that the Democrats would unite to defeat Lincoln. He felt that any other result would mean the death of the Union.

The election of Abraham Lincoln as president in November 1860 and the news that South Carolina had voted to secede sent a wave of pro-secession feeling rolling through Texas. With the Lone Star flag sprouting up everywhere, Lee withdrew into himself and nursed an agonizing fear that his home state of Virginia might also secede, forcing him to make a choice between the state he loved and the country he served. Lee felt that Virginia claimed his first loyalty. In a letter to his son Rooney, he wrote, "If the Union is dissolved and the government disrupted, I shall return to my native state and share the miseries of my people and save in her defence will draw my sword no more." In December, Lee left San Antonio to take command of the Second Cavalry at nearby Fort Mason. He and the men in his command went through the motions of performing their duties. Everyone felt caught in a haze of unreality as reports of more states leaving the Union shattered their familiar world into pieces around them. At the end of January 1861, a Texas convention voted to secede and join South Carolina, Georgia, Florida, Alabama, Mississippi, and Louisiana in setting up a new Southern nation. On February 4, a convention in Montgomery, Alabama, elected Jefferson Davis president of the Confederate States of America. That same day, Lee received orders to get out of Texas and report to General Scott in Washington. As Lee climbed into an army ambulance to begin his journey, a young officer shouted out, "Colonel, do you intend to go south or remain north?" Lee responded with a sentence that betrayed the bitter sense of divided loyalty he felt: "I shall never bear arms against the Union, but it may be necessary for me to carry a musket in defense of my native state Virginia, in which case I shall not prove recreant to my duty."

Under orders from Jefferson Davis to attack Fort Sumter before it could be reinforced by federal troops, General Pierre Gustave Toutant Beauregard initiated the bombardment that formally began the Civil War. In the 33-hour assault, his troops spent 4,000 shells before the Union garrison surrendered.

Lee reported at the War Department on March 5. He told General Scott that although he did not believe in either secession or slavery, he did not have it in him to fight against Virginia should she secede. Lee then returned to Arlington and waited for the situation to develop. When on March 28 the War Department offered him command of the First Cavalry, Lee immediately accepted, hoping against hope that he could remain in the army. On April 12, Confederate batteries opened fire on Fort Sumter, in the harbor at Charleston, South Carolina, which Lincoln had refused to hand over to the South Carolina authorities. When the fort surrendered, the president issued a call for 75,000 volunteers to put down in his words "combinations . . . too powerful to be suppressed by the ordinary course of judicial proceedings." The American Civil War had begun.

Meanwhile, General Scott worked behind the scenes in Washington to try to hold his favorite officer for the Union. Lincoln gave his consent to a plan to offer Lee the post of general in chief of the Union armies and ordered the Washington politician Francis Blair to "ascertain Lee's intentions and feelings." On April 18, Blair invited Lee to his house and proposed that he take over the command of all

Southern unionists hold a secret meeting during the American Civil War. Lee was among many other Southerners who did not believe that secession was in the South's — or the country's — best interest but who fought for the South nonetheless.

This advertisement was run to announce the publication of the Confederate national anthem, "God Save the South," in 1862. During the American Civil War, a sense of purpose bolstered the South, and its people were willing to make great sacrifices for what they referred to as "the cause."

Federal forces gathering to suppress the Southern revolt. Lee listened quietly and then politely declined, saying that he could take no part in an invasion of the South. When he left the Blair house, Lee went directly to General Scott's office and told his mentor of his decision. The dismayed Scott responded, "Lee, you have made the greatest mistake of your life; but I feared it would be so." The two men discussed the situation for a while before Scott said sadly, "If you propose to resign, it is proper that you should do so at once. Your present attitude is equivocal." Lee knew full well that he could no longer continue in the U.S. Army in time of war if he refused to accept postings. He returned to Arlington amid rumors that Virginia had passed an ordinance of secession in response to Lincoln's call for state troops to help suppress the revolt. On April 20, when all doubt in Lee's mind that Virginia would leave the Union had passed, he drafted a letter to Secretary of War Simon Cameron, resigning his commission as colonel of the First Cavalry.

4

Behind the Scenes

Gloom filled the mansion at Arlington after Lee dispatched his letter of resignation. No one in the household shared in the public elation at Virginia's secession. The next day, April 21, Lee and his family traveled to Alexandria to attend church. As the son of Light-Horse Harry rode through the town, the eyes of many of Alexandria's inhabitants followed him questioningly. Most people in the area regarded Lee as George Washington's heir and therefore Virginia's natural protector. The Alexandria *Gazette* had openly issued a call for him to command Virginia's military forces. Now everyone waited anxiously to hear what he would do.

Lee received a letter that evening inviting him to the state capital for a conference with the governor. The next day he caught the southbound train to Richmond. At each stop along the way cheering crowds demanded that he come out and address them. On his arrival Lee found Richmond in a state of combined excitement and panic. The news of the arrival of the Confederate vice-president, Alexander

Trusting in Almighty God, an approving conscience, and the aid of my fellow citizens, I devote myself to the service of my native state, in whose behalf alone will I ever again draw my sword.
—ROBERT E. LEE

A hospital for Confederate officers in Richmond, Virginia, during the 1860s. From the very first Civil War battles, the nation had to face the grim reality of armed conflict — the casualties. For instance, at the First Battle of Manassas, nearly 5,000 men were killed or wounded.

Stephens, to negotiate the union of Virginia with the Confederate States competed on the streets with rumors of a Federal warship steaming up the James River to bombard the city. Lee went immediately to see the governor, John Letcher, who promptly offered him command of all the armed forces in the state, with the accompanying rank of major general. Bowing to the dictates of his sense of duty, Lee accepted.

The next morning, Lee opened a tiny office near Richmond's Capitol Square. After addressing the Virginia Convention, he visited Stephens and assured him that he would have no problems operating under Confederate command if Virginia decided to join the rest of the South. He then turned his attention to the problems of defending his state. Although thousands of volunteers streamed into recruitment centers, the Virginia government had almost no guns or artillery with which to arm them and not enough ammunition to allow target practice. The hastily organized commissary department could provide little in the way of tents, backpacks, cartridge boxes, or even flags for the troops. Lee refused to do more than deploy the men and equipment he could muster in the defense of strategic points, despite almost overwhelming public sentiment for a quick offensive against the North. Militia units had managed to seize the arsenal at Harpers Ferry along with its weapons manufacturing machinery, but not before the Federal garrison had destroyed most of the guns stored there. Lee put Thomas J. Jackson, a professor from the Virginia Military Institute (VMI), in charge of protecting the town and its precious armaments industry and gave him as many men and guns as he could spare. The U.S. Navy had also destroyed most of the great naval base at Norfolk, downstream from Richmond at the entrance to Chesapeake Bay, but not without leaving much of value, including scuttled warships that could be raised and repaired. Lee put former U.S. Navy officers and engineers to work creating a fleet and blocking river access to the interior of the state. Meanwhile, with the help of VMI cadets, Lee set up training camps to drill the incoming volunteers as best he could.

As I think both sides are wrong in this fratricidal war, there is nothing comforting even in the hope that God may prosper the right, for there is no right in the matter.

—MARY CUSTIS LEE

On May 24, Union forces crossed the Potomac and occupied Alexandria and Arlington. Mary Lee packed up her valuables and left her childhood home, becoming one of the South's many upper-class refugees. At about the same time, the government of the Confederate States accepted Virginia's offer to move its capital from Montgomery to Richmond. This transfer of the seat of government placed the nerve center of the Confederacy only 100 miles from the federal capital at Washington and virtually guaranteed that northern and eastern Virginia would become the focal point of the war.

At the beginning of June, Lee turned command of all the armed forces in Virginia over to the Confederate government. When Davis arrived in Richmond, he kept Lee near him as his military adviser. Three weeks later, Union and Confederate armies clashed in front of Manassas Junction, less than 30 miles southwest of Washington. Lee had to wait out the battle in Richmond while Davis oversaw the action in person. Lee's old friend Joe Johnston, who had joined the Confederate army and taken com-

Southern refugees. As Union forces moved south, taking territory as they went, many Southerners were displaced from their homes. Packing whatever belongings they could onto rickety horse-drawn wagons, they moved their families, at least temporarily, out of harm's way.

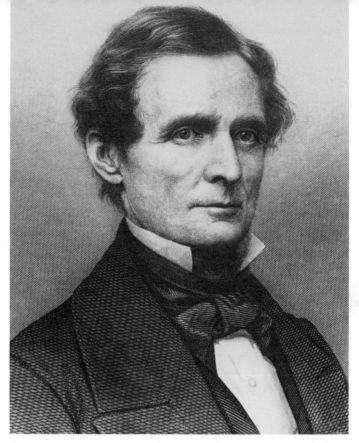

Jefferson Davis of Mississippi, a West Point graduate and a hero in the Mexican War, was elected to Congress in 1845. After establishing himself as a leader of the secessionist movement, he became president of the Confederacy — and Lincoln's nemesis — in 1861.

mand at Harpers Ferry, united his men with the force at Manassas commanded by General P. G. T. Beauregard. The two generals managed to send inexperienced Federal recruits reeling back toward Washington in panic, aided by a brigade under T. J. Jackson's command, which by standing firm at a dangerous moment earned its leader the nickname Stonewall. The Southern public made heroes out of Johnston, Beauregard, and Jackson; Lee, however, remained unrecognized behind the scenes, grateful that his dispositions had stood the test of combat.

After the Battle of Manassas, Davis sent Lee into the mountains of western Virginia, where Federal troops, marching southeast through the Allegheny Mountains, threatened to cut the railroads leading from Virginia to the western states of the Confederacy, block access to the Shenandoah Valley, and cut off Harpers Ferry and Manassas from Richmond. Davis gave Lee the almost impossible task of coordinating the three Confederate armies in the area without placing him in actual field command.

Lee set out in July through the mountains to see what he could do. He found the soldiers exhausted and demoralized, both by Federal attacks and by steady rain, and suffering from starvation due to a poor supply organization. Rain drenched supplies of gunpowder and turned roads into seas of mud. Officers found excuses for disobeying orders and often ignored Lee when he tried to get them to move their units. The commanders of two of the armies on the scene refused to cooperate, each claiming authority over the other. Lee, facing jealousy and ineptitude for the first time in his military career and hampered by his lack of formal authority, tried unsuccessfully to govern the situation with tactful suggestion and gentlemanly prods at honor. Only after Davis stepped in and removed one of the commanders did Lee manage to unite all three armies and halt the Federal advance. All attempts to take the offensive, however, ended in failure.

The Virginian public reacted with shock and scorn to the debacle. People who had expected miracles from the son of Light-Horse Harry held Lee personally responsible for the failure to drive the Federals out of western Virginia. Newspaper editors wrote blistering editorials, and people began referring to their former hero as Granny Lee. Lee patiently bore the attacks, but in a letter to Mary he vented his bitterness: "I know [the newspaper editors] can regulate matters satisfactorily to themselves on paper. I wish they could do so in the field." Jefferson Davis knew what Lee had faced and continued to trust him. When the U.S. Navy began to threaten the lightly defended coast of South Carolina, Davis created a military department to cover the Atlantic coast from South Carolina to Florida and placed Lee in command. Lee did not want the job. He had pledged to defend Virginia, not South Carolina, and he saw the defense of long stretches of coastline against the might of the Federal navy as yet another forlorn assignment where a good man might fail through no fault of his own. The South Carolinians, however, welcomed Lee with open arms. Light-Horse Harry still loomed large in Carolinian mythology, and the people gladly saw his son placed in charge of their defense.

Lee found his worst expectations fulfilled. On November 7, a Federal fleet captured the forts guarding Port Royal, at the southern tip of South Carolina between Charleston and Savannah, Georgia, and landed an army of 12,000 men. Port Royal Sound provided entrance to a vast maze of inland waterways that penetrated deep into the interior of the state. With gunboats able to sail these waters at will and a large army ashore, the Federals could drive deeply into the flank of the Confederacy with very little opposition. In a report to Richmond, Lee wrote, "The strength of the enemy . . . exceeds the whole force we have in the state; it can be thrown with great celerity against any point, and far outnumbers any force we can bring against it in the field." Taking command more firmly than he had in West Virginia, Lee worked frantically to improve the defenses of Charleston and Savannah and set militia units to work building sophisticated field fortifications to protect the railroad connecting them. He had to fight against a shortage of arms and ammunition, the panic of local residents, and the reluctance of the South Carolina and Georgia governors to allow state troops to operate under Confederate command. The young volunteers that Lee put to work digging trenches grumbled at the unexpected manual labor. Their reluctance to dig and the slow pace of the work frustrated Lee, who wrote caustically that he hoped "our enemy will be polite enough to wait for us." Surprisingly enough, Union forces cooperated. Federal commanders could not figure out what to do with their success, giving Lee enough time to make the region secure.

In early 1862, Jefferson Davis, in a political maneuver aimed at frustrating attempts in the Confederate Congress to supplant him with a professional commander in chief, recalled Lee to Richmond to act under presidential direction as director of military operations throughout the Confederacy. When he arrived at the Confederate capital in March, Lee found the situation in Virginia to be grim. The Confederacy had a total of less than 60,000 men in the entire state. On the outskirts of Washington, the vain and ambitious General

George B. McClellan, who had served on Lee's engineering staff in Mexico, prepared a Federal army of more than twice that number for an attack on Richmond. The Confederates had their forces deployed in a broad semicircle stretching from the Shenandoah Valley to Norfolk, headed by Joe Johnston, with 30,000 men lined along the Rappahannock River. Lee spent the first few weeks in March acting as a liaison between Johnston and Davis, who did not trust each other, and taking care of the administration of other armies in the Confederacy. On March 20, however, he received word that Union troops had arrived at the Federal-held Fort Monroe. Both Yorktown and Fort Monroe lay on the Peninsula, a stretch of thickly wooded, rolling countryside running between the York and the James rivers from Chesapeake Bay to Richmond. Lee could not tell whether the news meant an attack on Norfolk or the Carolinas or a march on Richmond. Lee asked Johnston to send some of his men to Yorktown. Johnston refused to divide his command. Lee resorted to quietly detaching troops in small numbers from Johnston and sending them to the Peninsula.

By mid-April it had become clear that McClellan had brought his Army of the Potomac to the Peninsula, and Davis ordered Johnston to bring his army southward and take command of Richmond's defense. When he arrived on the scene, Johnston recommended concentrating all available forces in front of the city for a showdown battle with McClellan. Lee successfully pressed the president instead to fight on the Peninsula in the hopes of buying time. He then began to work without consulting Davis. He worried about the Union army corps of 33,000 men under General Irvin McDowell that remained in front of Washington. This force would almost certainly march south to join McClellan and put Johnston's army in a vise from north and east that it could not withstand. Only 2,500 soldiers at Fredericksburg, on the Rappahannock River, stood in McDowell's way. Lee began detaching small units from armies in other states and sending them to Fredericksburg. He also opened quiet communications with Stonewall Jackson,

Joseph Eggleston Johnston, a classmate of Lee's at West Point, also served in the Mexican War with distinction. As a Confederate general, Johnston was outmaneuvered by Grant at Vicksburg and later surrendered to General William T. Sherman.

General Thomas "Stonewall" Jackson led Confederate troops in a rout of Union forces at Manassas Junction, Virginia, on July 21, 1861, and to a number of other victories during the first two years of the war. He was fatally wounded by one of his own men in 1863.

commanding a small force of 8,000 men in the Shenandoah Valley. On April 21, Lee sent a letter to Jackson suggesting that he gather scattered Confederate forces in the valley and strike northward for the Potomac River in a bid to frighten Lincoln into holding McDowell's corps for the defense of Washington. Jackson pounced on Lee's suggestion. He broke all contact with Richmond and quietly marched up the valley to see if he could stir up any mischief.

On May 1, Lee learned that the Confederate army on the Peninsula had evacuated Yorktown. Johnston stopped communicating with his superiors, and Lee could only gather from rumors of pitched battles in the pouring rain that his old friend continued to contest General McClellan's advance. By May 22, Johnston had fallen back to the Chickahominy River, the last natural barrier in front of Richmond. Parts of his line lay almost within the city's northeastern suburbs. Although Lee strengthened the city's defenses as best he could, his thoughts anxiously traveled with Jackson's troops, out of touch somewhere in the Shenandoah Valley. If Jackson failed, only a miracle could prevent McDowell from joining with McClellan. The dreaded news that only 25 miles separated the 2 Federal forces came on May 26, as did the hoped-for dispatch from the valley. Jackson's men, carrying little more than their muskets, had made an incredible series of rapid marches, earning themselves the name "Jackson's foot cavalry." In a series of swift battles, Jackson had thrown the Union forces facing him into panic and had sent a large Federal army reeling back in disarray toward Washington. He had managed to penetrate as far as Harpers Ferry and retreat again before the stunned Federals could unite to crush him. Lee could now only pray that Jackson's dazzling performance would induce Lincoln to pull McDowell's corps back.

General Johnston announced his intent to attack the Army of the Potomac on May 29. When the day arrived, Lee found to his surprise that no attack had taken place. He rushed on horseback to the front lines, to be greeted by the news that his miracle had happened. Cavalry units under Jeb Stuart reported that McDowell had halted his troops in the road and turned them back toward Washington. Johnston postponed his attack for two days after hearing the news. Lee, frustrated by serving as an administrator during a time of crisis, sent a note to Johnston asking to serve in the field in any capacity. Johnston sent a polite reply but betrayed nothing of his battle plans. On May 31, Lee set out with some of his lieutenants to the front. He located Johnston at his advanced headquarters. His friend seemed preoccupied and did not clarify his plan of attack. That afternoon, the two men heard gunfire, and Lee saw Confederate soldiers hurrying forward. Shortly afterward, Davis appeared, prompting Johnston to ride off to avoid meeting him. As the sounds of battle swelled, Davis and Lee decided to ride to the front themselves to find out what they could. With afternoon turning to evening, Davis, tall and hawklike, and Lee, sporting a full gray beard he had grown while in western Virginia, rode along a road between an open field and thick woods. They soon found themselves in the thick of battle. On both sides of them, Confederate infantry struggled through the trees, trying to get at their opponents, as well-placed Federal artillery poured out a merciless fire. The president tried to give orders to help the situation but could not find any senior officers. With darkness falling, the exhausted survivors fell back. A courier rushed up to Davis and Lee with news that Johnston had been wounded, possibly fatally. The arrival of an ambulance with the wounded general confirmed the news. Lee and Davis at last located the senior surviving Confederate general, who nervously promised not to retreat the next day. Turning back to the city, they rode quietly in the darkness along an endless line of ambulance wagons. At length Davis said, "General Lee, I shall assign you to the command of this army. Make your preparations as soon as you reach your quarters. I shall send you the order when we get to Richmond."

If there is any man in either army head and shoulders above every other in audacity, it is General Lee! . . . He will take more desperate chances and take them quicker than any other general in this country, north or south.

—JOSEPH IVES
Confederate colonel

5

The Army of Northern Virginia

Jefferson Davis had at long last given Lee the chance to lead his own army in the field. In an address to the troops announcing his assumption of command, Lee gave clear notice of what he intended to do. He referred to his men as the Army of Northern Virginia, an indication that he did not intend to remain on the defensive any longer than absolutely necessary. He believed that the Confederate army belonged in northern Virginia, but to lead his troops north he first had to dislodge General McClellan's massive army from Richmond's doorstep.

Lee ordered his soldiers to dig a huge system of earthworks and trenches in front of the city. He planned to leave a small force behind these fortifications to defend the city while he took the bulk of the army out to maneuver for an attack. The men grumbled at the work, and the Richmond press had a field day, giving Lee in addition to the usual Granny the new title of the King of Spades, but Lee ignored the complaints and the ridicule.

The mental strain was so great that I saw at that moment the singular effect mentioned, I think, in the life of Goethe on a similar occasion—the whole landscape for an instant turned slightly red.
—Union soldier after the Battle of Sharpsburg

Lee's brilliance on the battlefield astounded both his enemies and his Confederate comrades, but he was not simply a cool, calculating military leader. Rather, he was a man of deep moral conviction with a great respect for human life.

On June 12, 1862, Lee sent Jeb Stuart with 1,200 of his cavalrymen on a spectacular ride all the way around the Union army that quickly enshrined Stuart as a Confederate hero. When he returned, Stuart revealed that the northern corps of McClellan's army had nothing protecting its right flank. An attacking army could with very little trouble march around the northern end of the Union army and cut its supply line to Fort Monroe, which ran eastward along the Richmond and York River Railroad to the Pamunkey River. With his communications cut, McClellan would have to retreat or face the destruction of his army. On the night of June 25, Lee wrote out orders for an attack the next day based on Stuart's information. He directed Stonewall Jackson and his triumphant but footsore force, which had begun to march toward Richmond two weeks previously, to swing around the unprotected northern flank of McClellan's army. Leaving 25,000 men holding the newly built earthworks in front of Richmond, Lee ordered the rest of his army, numbering just over 41,000 men, to cross the Chickahominy River and assault the Federal line. With Jackson in his rear, McClellan would have no choice but to pull the right side of his army back across the river. Nothing would then stand in the way of the Army of Northern Virginia and the Federal supply line. If Lee played his cards right, he could completely cut off the Union army, destroy it, and win the war at a stroke. One great danger existed, however. If McClellan realized how few men guarded the works in front of Richmond, he could assault the fortifications with overwhelming numbers and easily capture the Confederate capital. Lee decided, however, that McClellan would never make such a bold move. Lee was gambling with the life of his country, and he knew it. If he had guessed wrongly, he could lose everything. He thought it better, however, to risk all to gain all rather than play it safe and wait for McClellan to lay siege to the city.

The last week of June 1862 quickly became enshrined in Confederate legend as the Seven Days. Lee's soldiers fought their way southeast against the resisting Union troops, through swamps and heav-

[It was] one gigantic twenty-mile-long conflict, with bewildering intermissions, not for resting, but for groping spastically in the general direction of an enemy who fought so savagely when cornered that the whole thing had rather been like playing blind man's bluff with a buzz saw.

—SHELBY FOOTE
Civil War historian, on the
Seven Days

ily wooded hills, in a long series
McClellan to abandon his supply
southward toward the James Riv
gunboats waited with their he
marshes and ravines of the Peninsul
staccato rattle of musket fire, the dul
non, and the high-pitched, bloodcurdli
Lee could not, however, manage to c
Clellan's retreat. His army had little e
fighting on the offensive. Regiments got lost,
assignments, or stood in the road while the
manders argued about who should go first. S
wall Jackson, on the Confederate left flank, sho
an inexplicable lack of energy that resulted in l
failure to get between the Army of the Potomac an
the James.

By the evening of June 30, McClellan's army had
reached Malvern Hill, a heavily wooded plateau less
than eight miles from Harrison's Landing on the
James River. Lee and some of his senior commanders discussed the possibilities of an attack. The aus-
tere and normally aggressive General Daniel H. Hill
warned against assaulting such a strong position.
The burly James "Old Pete" Longstreet ridiculed Hill
for his caution. When Jubal Early, a brigadier general from the West Virginia mountains, commented
that McClellan might get away, Lee lost his temper.
He burst out angrily, "Yes, he will get away because
I cannot have my orders carried out!" Feeling that
he had to strike one last blow, Lee ordered an assault
of Malvern Hill for July 1. But Confederate artillery
failed to silence the grim rows of Federal cannon
drawn up on the crest of the hill, units jumped off
late, and the attack, when it finally started up the
slope, ended in a bloody failure. That evening, as
the twinkling lights of field hospitals cut through
the darkness and the desperate cries of wounded
men sounded from the hillside, McClellan's army
escaped.

Despite the confusion in his army that had enabled the Federal army to get away, Lee had managed to break McClellan's grip on Richmond and
badly maul his troops. The tired men of the Army
of Northern Virginia began to cheer him enthusi-

...lly whenever he rode by, and the Richmond press changed its tune and hailed him as the city's savior. The victory had, however, cost the Confederacy dearly. More than 3,000 men were killed in Lee's army, and some 15,000 were wounded, totaling nearly one-quarter of the entire army. Observers began to notice that Lee rarely laughed anymore and that his dark brown eyes reflected a deep sadness. Despite his losses, however, Lee had to capitalize on what he had won. He had long cherished the idea of invading the Northern states. During Jackson's valley campaign, Lee had noted how sensitively President Lincoln had reacted to any threat to the Federal capital. If Lee could take his army into Maryland and Pennsylvania, he might throw Lincoln off balance, disrupt any plans the Federals might have, and demonstrate to the Northern people that the attempt to suppress the South could only lead to a long, expensive war on their own soil. He had to act quickly, however. A new commander, Major General John Pope, had taken command of Union forces in the Shenandoah Valley and united them into the Army of Virginia, numbering over 50,000 men. If Pope and McClellan began to march on Richmond at the same time, they could concentrate some 140,000 men against the less than 80,000 Lee could assemble.

Gambling once more that McClellan would not react aggressively, Lee sent Stonewall Jackson on July 13 with 12,000 soldiers to the railroad junction town of Gordonsville, 65 miles northwest of Richmond and 25 miles south of Pope's army. McClellan rewarded Lee's trust. He remained immobile on the James, badgering Washington for reinforcements. Lee then took a longer chance and sent A. P. Hill with his division of 17,000 to join Jackson. On August 13, Lee committed himself totally by sending Longstreet with 25,000 men to join Jackson. Two days later, Lee left his last 25,000 men guarding Richmond and headed north himself. As he departed, the beaten Army of the Potomac packed its bags and withdrew from the Peninsula, leaving Richmond secure from attack from the east.

> *Lee seldom got into personal vendettas, but he made an exception with Pope. He could hardly pronounce the man's name, his anger against him was so great.*
>
> —JOHN BOWERS
> American author, on Lee's adversary at the Second Battle of Manassas

An attempt on August 18 to get behind Pope's army and cut his supply line failed when a Federal patrol captured a copy of Lee's orders. Pope retreated hastily across the Rappahannock, and the frustrated Lee waited for another opportunity. Advance elements of the Army of the Potomac landed two days later at Aquia Creek near Fredericksburg and began to march west to join Pope. By August 25, Pope had some 70,000 men against Lee's 55,000 and within a week could expect the rest of McClellan's army to join him.

Lee sent Jackson off to the northwest, behind the Bull Run Mountains, on a mission to get between Pope's army and Washington and provoke the Federal commander into retreating northward. The danger lay in that Pope, if he got wind of Lee's intentions, could strike the pieces of his army one at a time and destroy them. Lee, however, had an even lower regard for General Pope than he had for McClellan. He decided that with the men remaining with him he could fool Pope into thinking that nothing had changed.

Like Lee, Major General Ambrose Powell Hill attended West Point and served under General Winfield Scott. He later led the assault on Beaver Dam Creek and played a major role in the clash at Antietam Creek in Maryland on September 17, 1862.

Jackson gathered his troops and vanished to the northwest. On August 25, Lee thought he detected signs of retreat from the Federals facing him. He now had to reunite with Jackson quickly. The next day, Lee set his men in motion along the path that Jackson had taken. Soon after the march began, a dispatch arrived with electrifying news: Jackson had driven his men more than 50 miles in 40 hours, had slipped across the Bull Run Mountains through a pass called Thoroughfare Gap, and had suddenly appeared 20 miles behind Pope's army. He destroyed Pope's railroad communications with Washington and captured a huge Federal supply dump at Manassas Junction. Lee pressed on, fully aware that Pope would pursue Jackson and hoping that his hard-driving lieutenant could hold on. Early in the

Union soldiers survey the devastation wrought on the railroad track and equipment by Stonewall Jackson's men at Manassas Junction. Besides plundering the many Union supply trains, the rebels also effectively cut supply lines and communication between there and Washington.

morning on August 29, Lee and Longstreet's corps of 30,000 men marched through Thoroughfare Gap and approached the old Manassas battlefield. Lee's arrival caught Pope by surprise. The Federal general barely managed to save his army from total destruction and, together with McClellan, retreated toward the safety of the Washington fortifications.

After notifying a jubilant Confederacy of his stunning victory in the Second Battle of Manassas, Lee wrote to President Davis on September 3, "The present seems the most propitious time since the commencement of the war for the Confederate Army to enter Maryland." On the surface, the Army of Northern Virginia seemed at best poorly prepared to take the war into Union territory. Some 9,000 of Lee's soldiers were killed, wounded, or missing on the

Major General George Brinton McClellan led the Union forces at the Battle of Antietam. Although the battle was fought in but a single day, it was the bloodiest day of the entire war. More than 20,000 casualties resulted, about half from each side.

plains of Manassas. The remaining 40 worn-out brigades had very little food and ammunition. All of the Confederate soldiers wore ragged clothing, and thousands had no shoes. Even the officers seemed unready; Stonewall Jackson had hurt himself in a fall, Longstreet had an infected foot, and Lee himself had injured both hands in an accident on his gray charger, Traveller. Nonetheless, Lee felt he had to capitalize immediately on his success. If the Army of Northern Virginia defeated McClellan on northern soil, Maryland might leave the Union, and the war could conceivably end.

Lee ordered his tired men northward. At the end of the first week in September, the army crossed the Potomac at White's Ford, 40 miles northwest of Washington. Despite their hunger and fatigue, the Confederate soldiers confidently splashed across the river. The few battered Confederate bands played "Maryland, My Maryland." One young observer of the threadbare procession later described

Lee's soldiers as "the dirtiest men I ever saw, a most ragged, lean and hungry set of wolves. . . . They were profane beyond belief and talked incessantly." Another complained that the army stank. Lee ordered his troops not to destroy any private property and to pay for any animals or supplies they took. He also wrote a proclamation to the inhabitants inviting them to join the rebel cause and promising complete freedom of speech. Despite this gloves-on treatment, the Marylanders showed no signs of much pro-Confederate feeling. Shopkeepers closed their stores, farmers locked their barns, and thousands waved the Stars and Stripes as Lee's army marched by.

On September 9, Lee wrote his Special Orders No. 191 detailing his plan of campaign. He sent Jackson to take care of 10,000 Federal troops at Harpers Ferry that posed a threat to the Confederate supply line. The rest of the army would head west across the South Mountain ridge toward Hagerstown, 24 miles north of Jackson's target. With South Mountain screening his movements from the Federals, Lee could safely wait for Jackson before launching the rest of his campaign. Lee ordered copies of the orders sent to Longstreet, Jackson, and D. H. Hill. Hill received an extra copy from Jackson and gave it to an aide, who wrapped his cigars in it and mislaid them in the confusion of the march. Four days later, a Federal private with the Army of the Potomac, which had marched westward in slow pursuit of Lee, found the cigars and sent them to McClellan's headquarters.

Lee soon received word from Jeb Stuart of a puzzlingly energetic advance by McClellan toward South Mountain. On September 14, McClellan struck Hill and Longstreet, who were guarding the South Mountain passes with 18,000 men, with overwhelming strength, forcing them to retreat leaving 2,700 casualties behind. Faced with the disruption of his entire plan of campaign and unable to explain this unusually vigorous action by McClellan, Lee saw no choice but to take the scattered units of his army back across the Potomac before McClellan could defeat them in detail. He ordered a retreat via the tiny town of Sharpsburg, 17 miles north of Harpers Ferry. On the morning of September 15, however, came invigorating news. Jackson had captured Harpers Ferry along with its entire garrison. With his communications secure, if Lee could concentrate his army quickly enough, he still might defeat the Army of the Potomac and continue his campaign. He sent orders for everybody to regroup at Sharpsburg as quickly as possible.

The orderly little town of Sharpsburg, surrounded by tidy, regular fields of ripening corn, lay on a broad slope. To the west, the ground rose for just over a mile to the banks of the Potomac; to the east the land sank down to a small stream running north-south called Antietam Creek. Lee arranged Hill and Longstreet's troops in a long line on the eastern edge of town. Shortly afterward, a sea of blue-clad soldiers some 88,000 strong came into view and drew up in a line facing Lee's. His old caution reasserting itself, McClellan decided to wait and observe Lee at just the moment of his greatest weakness. The wait continued throughout the foggy day of September 16. Stonewall Jackson, who had left A. P. Hill guarding Harpers Ferry with 5,000 men, arrived, and his men trickled into place on the north end of Lee's line, gradually pushing Lee's complement to more than 30,000. Shortly before sunset, the Federals tested Jackson's strength, giving Lee a hint about where McClellan intended to strike. A counterattack led by a brigade of Texans under General John Hood threw the Union soldiers back.

On the misty dawn of September 17, Federal cannon opened fire with a shattering roar. Long, disciplined rows of Union infantry marched through a cornfield in front of Jackson's position and struck savagely at his line. Again Hood's Texans, giving vent to the rebel yell, led a countercharge. As the battle raged among the cornstalks, Lee rode from brigade to brigade encouraging the men. He also sent word to Harpers Ferry for A. P. Hill to bring his men to the scene as quickly as possible. Charge gave way to countercharge as the morning turned clear and fair. The fighting in front of Jackson's line finally died down about noon, leaving 13,000 dead and wounded from both sides heaped up between the 2 armies. As an uneasy silence settled over the field, Lee rode to the Sixth Alabama Regiment, in front of D. H. Hill's corps in the center. He leaned down and told the regiment's commander, John Gordon, that the line must be held at all costs. As Lee rode off, Gordon replied, "These men are going to stay here, General, till the sun goes down or victory is won."

Shortly afterward, fresh Union soldiers, in new blue uniforms with white gaiters on their boots, filed across the creek and formed an assault column four lines deep. The Stars and Stripes waved bravely, and as a band in the rear played march music, the Federal column moved with parade-ground precision into a charge. Gordon's Alabamans decimated the oncoming soldiers, but the Federals regrouped and charged again. Lee rode back and forth behind his hard-pressed center, rallying his troops. The line nearly broke. D. H. Hill shouldered a musket, and Longstreet had his staff working artillery pieces. Lee remained calm and shuttled men from one part of the line to meet each new Federal charge.

Early that afternoon, the Federal attacks died down, leaving Lee's center buckled but not broken. A new assault quickly opened up on Longstreet's corps, on the south end of Lee's line, which had been weakened to send reinforcements to Jackson and Hill. After only a couple of hours, Longstreet's men had reached their limit, and the situation seemed hopeless. Lee spotted a rising dust cloud to the southeast and asked a subordinate what he saw. The officer replied that he saw the Stars and Stripes. Lee next directed the lieutenant's attention to another cloud of dust rising to the southwest. The man replied excitedly that he saw the flags of Virginia and the Confederacy. Without betraying his relief, Lee said quietly, "It is A. P. Hill from Harpers Ferry." Hill had driven his men at a near run for 17 miles. Some 2,000 of them had dropped back exhausted, but 3,000 still came on. Without stopping, Hill's men cut loose with the rebel yell and smashed into the south end of the Federal line. The stunned

A doctor cares for wounded Confederate soldiers in the aftermath of the Battle of Antietam. Of the 75,000 Union soldiers and 52,000 Confederates who fought in the battle, more than 4,000 were killed and some 19,000 wounded.

Union soldiers broke into little knots of men fighting desperately for survival and fled the field, leaving Longstreet's line intact.

Evening fell, and the battle sputtered to a close. Lee called in his senior generals for a conference. Everyone had gloomy tales to tell. The Army of Northern Virginia had held the field, but just barely. One-fourth of the entire army had fallen, and only 26,000 men remained fit to fight. Everyone expressed a desire to retreat. To his subordinates' shocked surprise, Lee declared his intention to stay and fight. McClellan had not used his overwhelming strength in a coordinated attack. If McClellan repeated his tactics, Lee felt that his men just might win a conclusive victory. The following day, as the

weary but determined Confederates waited and watched the Union lines, the dead horses and men in between the two armies swelled slowly in the sun, and the wounded cried out for water. McClellan, whose army had also suffered, remained motionless. As night fell, Lee decided to retreat. His soldiers lit campfires and abandoned them, stealing off quietly during the night. Lee rode down to the Potomac and sat on his horse in the stream while the advance units waded across. The rear guard of the army found Lee in the same spot the next morning. Lee asked the unit's commander for news. The officer replied that the entire army had safely reached Virginia soil. "Thank God," Lee replied, and turned his horse southward.

6

In a Blaze of Glory

At first Lee did not regard the Battle of Antietam as more than a temporary check. Soon after the battle he began to sketch a plan to recross the Potomac. Only as reports began to filter into his headquarters about the condition of his army did Lee realize the extent of the blow he had taken. On September 22, Lee could count on only 36,418 men, and most of those had no shoes or blankets and only ragged clothing. Thousands of Confederate stragglers and deserters stole through the woods and fields of northern Virginia, trying to avoid patrols sent to round them up. Lee reluctantly abandoned his hopes for a renewed offensive and pulled his army back into the upper Shenandoah Valley for much needed rest and reorganization.

On October 20, fate dealt Lee a harsh personal blow when his youngest daughter, Annie, died of diphtheria. In a letter to Mary, Lee wrote, "To know that I shall never see her again on earth, that her place in our circle, which I always hoped one day to enjoy, is vacant, is agonizing in the extreme."

I never in my life felt more certain that I was doing right than I do in signing this paper.
—ABRAHAM LINCOLN
on signing the Emancipation Proclamation

The remains of a Confederate blockade runner off the South Carolina coast. Nearly invisible at night, blockade runners were used to slip undetected through enemy squadrons. When spotted and pursued, however, the vessels were usually run onto shoals or demolished by enemy fire.

General Ambrose Burnside, whose forces were defeated by Lee at Fredericksburg. The Union general will likely be remembered more for his style of facial hair — sideburns — than for any military feats he accomplished.

On October 26, Lee received word that McClellan had crossed the Potomac. So, with the Army of Northern Virginia once more in fighting trim, he put his men on the march. Leaving Jackson in the upper valley, Lee took Longstreet's First Corps, now containing roughly half of the Army, south to the town of Culpeper, 30 miles northeast of Fredericksburg, to block any advance on Richmond east of the Blue Ridge Mountains. In early November, the waiting Confederates learned that Lincoln had relieved McClellan and placed Major General Ambrose E. Burnside at the head of the Army of the Potomac. On hearing of the removal of his old adversary, Lee remarked to Longstreet, "We understood each other so well. I fear they may continue to make these changes till they find someone whom I don't understand."

Burnside quickly advanced on Fredericksburg. Lee set Longstreet in motion to block him. The ancient town offered a perfect location for Lee to receive Burnside's attack. Behind the town to the south and west, a long rampart of low ridges and wooded hills provided an ideal defensive position on which the Army of the Potomac could well break its back. When Joe Johnston, in Tennessee on a tour of inspection with Davis, heard that Burnside had marched on the city, he remarked wryly, "What luck some people have. Nobody will ever come to attack me in such a place." Lee ordered Jackson to join him at Fredericksburg before the rapidly advancing winter halted travel. On December 13, Burnside sent his men up the heights in several futile attempts to break the Confederate army. Lee could not believe that the Federal general had handed him such a perfect opportunity for an easy victory. He remarked exultantly to Longstreet, "It is well that war is so terrible —we should grow too fond of it."

Despite the easy triumph, Lee was depressed. He had not managed to bring about the sort of battle that would destroy the Federal army and win the war. He decided to keep his army at Fredericksburg for the winter. When spring came, he could make another attempt to find the decisive victory that had eluded him for so long.

The winter of 1862–63 soon proved to be one of the coldest in Virginia's history. Lee's soldiers huddled in their camps around Fredericksburg, shivering, without coats, blankets, tents, shoes, or even underwear. As the months progressed, food supplies began to run low. Lee made desperate appeals to Richmond for aid, but Davis could do little. Although the Confederacy had ample stockpiles of meat and grain, it could not get the food to its principal army because the Southern railroad network, lightly built to begin with, could not handle the demands of wartime.

By the middle of February 1863, Lee had to admit that with the army in such miserable condition and the roads muddy and impassable, he could not immediately take the offensive. He sent Longstreet's corps south to meet a threat from Federal troops massing at Norfolk and, incidentally, to gather supplies to keep the rest of the army alive. The pressures and anxieties of life on the Rappahannock that year took their toll on Lee. On March 30, he became ill and was forced to spend the first two weeks of April in a farmhouse bed.

Former slaves wait for Emancipation Day festivities to begin in front of a store decorated for the occasion with a Lincoln portrait. After Lincoln signed the Emancipation Proclamation on January 1, 1863, one Philadelphia lawyer said, "Joy fills my soul at the prospect of the future. . . . In spirit and in purpose, thanks to Almighty God, this is no longer a slaveholding republic."

General Joseph Hooker. Lincoln appointed Fighting Joe to take command of the Army of the Potomac, but his defeat at Chancellorsville proved he was as ineffective as McLellan and Burnside before him.

As spring broke along the Rappahannock, the convalescent Lee could finally turn his thoughts to the offensive. He had not given up his dream of invading the North. The Federals, however, forced Lee to begin the season's campaigning on the defensive. On April 30, the Army of the Potomac, which Lincoln had taken from Burnside and given to General Joseph "Fighting Joe" Hooker, crossed the Rapidan River west of Fredericksburg and marched south. Lee left some 10,000 men to guard Fredericksburg and took the remaining 46,000 with him toward the tiny village of Chancellorsville, near the junction of the Rapidan and the upper Rappahannock.

Chancellorsville provided almost ideal conditions for a smaller army to contest the advance of a larger one. Running south from the Rapidan ran an area known as the Wilderness, a rolling, densely forested belt of almost impenetrable thickets choked with undergrowth. On May 1, after a seemingly irresistible advance, Hooker's army moved into the Wilderness, made a few tentative thrusts against Lee's lines, and then, for no apparent reason, retreated.

Lee, guessing that the new Union commander had lost his nerve and with it his control of the battle, decided to risk once more his favorite ploy. After learning from Jeb Stuart's cavalry that the western end of the Federal line simply petered out into the woods with no protection, he ordered Stonewall Jackson to take his 28,000 men on a long, circling march to take advantage of Hooker's carelessness. Only 14,000 soldiers remained facing the entire Army of the Potomac. Jackson started his men off at dawn on May 2, marched them 14 miles through the woods, and came screaming with explosive force into the unprepared Federal right. Hooker's troops were preparing dinner when a rush of terrified wild animals followed by a line of screaming rebel soldiers tore through their encampment. The entire right side of Hooker's line crumpled, forcing him to retreat more than two miles by dusk.

That night, Jackson rode out with members of his staff to scout out the Federal position. Nervous Confederates opened fire on the returning party, hitting Jackson in the left arm. Lee turned command of the Second Corps over to Jeb Stuart. The flamboyant cavalryman led Jackson's men in an attack through the burning woods that pushed the Federals into a confused, frightened mass with their backs to the river.

Lee rode north to view the results for himself. His secretary, Charles Marshall, recorded the event: "The fierce soldiers with their faces blackened with the smoke of battle, the wounded crawling with feeble limbs from the fury of the devouring flames, all seemed possessed with a common impulse. One long, unbroken cheer . . . rose high above the roar of battle, and hailed the presence of the victorious chief. [Lee] sat in the full realization of all that soldiers dream of—triumph."

Lee did not have much leisure to bask in the glow of success. On May 10, Stonewall Jackson died, leaving Lee forever robbed of his right-hand man. He also had to contend with attempts in Richmond to take part of his army and send it west to fight a Federal advance along the Mississippi River. Lee traveled to Richmond in mid-May to argue in front

Lee knew what this wound meant. Stonewall had lost his left arm; but . . . Lee had lost his right.
—EUGENE SMITH
in *Lee and Grant*

of the Confederate cabinet for his cherished northern offensive and prevent the weakening of his forces. He won his case, largely because his prestige and that of his army had reached unprecedented heights. Lee and others had begun to believe that the Army of Northern Virginia could not be beaten.

On his return to Fredericksburg, Lee reorganized the army again, this time into three corps, retaining Longstreet in command of the First Corps and creating a new Third Corps for A. P. Hill. He gave command of Jackson's old Second Corps to Major General Richard Ewell, a cavalryman who had lost a leg at the Second Battle of Manassas. Lee set his army in motion up the Shenandoah Valley on June 13. He felt anxious not knowing whether the Army of the Potomac had crossed the Potomac ahead of him. On June 22, he sent orders to Jeb Stuart to find out and to remain in close contact with Ewell's troops. Unknown to Lee, the vainglorious Stuart,

Confederate general Richard Stoddert Ewell served under Stonewall Jackson during the Shenandoah Valley campaign. After Jackson was mortally wounded in the Battle of Chancellorsville, Lee placed Jackson's corps in Ewell's hands.

who had been badly surprised by a Federal cavalry attack near Culpeper early in the month, decided to recapture his lost prestige by repeating his famous ride around the Union army. He disobeyed Lee's directive and headed east.

As the Army of Northern Virginia marched on into southern Pennsylvania, the soldiers were awed by the rich, rolling fields, bursting grain silos, and fat farm animals. Quartermasters fanned out to gather in the riches. On June 28, Lee finally heard from a spy that elements of the Union army had crossed the Potomac and reached Frederick, Maryland. The spy also reported that General George G. Meade, a former comrade of Lee's from the Mexican War, had replaced Hooker as the Army of the Potomac's commander. Lee ordered his scattered forces to concentrate near the little Pennsylvania town of Gettysburg, nestled in hilly country about seven miles north of the Maryland border. But he still had no word from Stuart and felt blinded to his enemy's whereabouts by the absence of his cavalry. On the evening of June 30, a courier brought word that men of A. P. Hill's Third Corps, foraging in Gettysburg for shoes, had stumbled into Federal troops. Lee had no idea, however, whether the men came from a detachment or the entire Army of the Potomac.

> The enemy is here, and if we do not whip him, he will whip us.
> —ROBERT E. LEE
> at Gettysburg

The next day, July 1, Lee headed east for Gettysburg, fretting angrily for Stuart. When he arrived, he found to his surprise units from the Third Corps, drawn up in a line across the road, in furious combat with Federal soldiers in place on the first of two long ridges rising west of the town. As he watched, the advance units of Ewell's Second Corps, arriving from the north and seeing the battle, charged into the right end of the Federal line. Lee saw a totally unplanned victory dropping into his lap and ordered the rest of the Third Corps to advance. After a desperate fight, the Federals broke and ran, heading through Gettysburg to take refuge on the high ground running south of the town. Lee rushed to the second of the two western ridges, Seminary Ridge, and scanned the scene. Immediately south of the town, a cleared rise called Cemetery Ridge

A Confederate soldier lies dead behind a barricade following the July 1863 Battle of Gettysburg. Jefferson Davis called the period following the defeat of Lee's Army of Northern Virginia by General George Gordon Meade's Army of the Potomac at Gettysburg as "the darkest hour of our political existence."

anchored the north end of a long stretch of high ground that bore the name Cemetery Hill. Toward the south end of Cemetery Ridge, two hills, called Big and Little Round Top, dominated the entire terrain. As the Federals rushed to take shelter, Lee sent word to Ewell to attack and take Cemetery Hill before the Federals could dig in. As he waited in growing bewilderment, nothing happened. With evening falling, an anxious Lee rode to the Second Corps headquarters. There he found that Ewell, overwhelmed by the responsibility of corps command, had failed to do anything.

Lee now faced a situation unlike any other since the war began. With the Federals fortifying the heights, he had to fight them on ground they had chosen. Without Stuart's troopers, he had no idea of Meade's dispositions and could not plan the sort of brilliant maneuvering that had won him the Seven Days and Chancellorsville. He finally resolved to mount a strong assault with the Second Corps from the north the following day while using newly arrived troops from Longstreet's First Corps to attack from the south, in the hopes of pushing the Federals off the high ground. The next morning,

feeling ill from a bout with diarrhea during the night, Lee put on his favorite black cavalry boots and a dress sword and joined his staff.

Longstreet, however, was reluctant to attack, not wanting to move until the last of his divisions came up, and he pressed Lee to adopt a completely different strategy. Observers noted a tense exchange between the two men before Lee headed for Ewell's headquarters, apparently believing that Longstreet would attack.

As two hours passed with no sign of Longstreet's attack, Lee grew visibly more anxious and irritated. At about noon, he rode back to Seminary Ridge to find the truculent Longstreet still waiting for his lost division. Almost frantic with impatience, Lee issued a flat order, and Longstreet put his corps in motion. By the time Longstreet launched his attack, the formerly empty southern end of Cemetery Hill swarmed with bluecoats. Nonetheless, Longstreet sent his men rushing up against the Federal defenses. Lee, sitting alone on a tree stump, could make out through his field glasses only the sparkle of musketry and sharp jabs of flame from cannon through the dense cloud of smoke as the two armies battled for control of the two Round Tops. Finally, at about dusk, he saw his men trickling back down the slope in defeat. Just as Longstreet's attack sputtered out, Ewell opened his assault from the north. For a brief moment several brigades under Jubal Early broke through to within yards of Meade's headquarters. As Federal troops massed for a counterattack, other Confederate units in front of the town that could have helped exploit the breakthrough moved too slowly. The Federal attack overwhelmed Early's men, slamming shut the door on an opportunity that might have won the day for the Confederacy.

That night, Lee sat alone in his tent. Some 9,000 Confederate soldiers had fallen for little gain. Yet he felt that he had to strike one more blow. Longstreet's final division, commanded by General George Pickett, was not far away. If Ewell made another attack from the north, a strong blow from Longstreet from the south might break the Federal line.

On the morning of July 3, Ewell lay ready to launch his diversion, but Lee could get no news of Longstreet or Pickett. When he finally located the commander of the First Corps, Lee found that Longstreet had not readied his men for their assault. Instead, he kept pushing for his own strategy. Lee finally got Longstreet to agree to move by giving in to his suggestion that the attack fall more in the center of Meade's line and to use Pickett's division together with troops of A. P. Hill's corps. He sent a message to Ewell to delay his attack, but the order arrived too late. Ewell, with an unusual display of vigor, had launched his attack, and Lee had lost all chance of making a coordinated assault. Though the First Corps had retreated in failure, Lee felt that he had to keep trying. As the morning progressed, the soldiers of Pickett's and Hill's command lay among the trees on Seminary Ridge and stared out at the heavily fortified heights, waiting for them across open fields over one-half mile away. Two cannon shots boomed out and shattered the stifling silence; 140 Confederate cannon, lined up wheel to wheel on Seminary Ridge, opened fire with a thunderous crash on the Federal positions; and Union

It's all my fault. I thought my men were invincible.

—ROBERT E. LEE
after Pickett's charge

artillery opened up in return. For two hours the heaviest artillery bombardment ever seen in North America raged. When the firing died down, 15,000 Confederate soldiers began to file out of the woods. The soldiers formed a line of 3 divisions, 2 in front and 1 in close support, more than half a mile long and 1,000 yards deep. Sunlight glittered off thousands of bayonets and musket barrels, and red Confederate battle flags fluttered in the breeze as the assault force formed its ranks. Then the gray divisions, the cream of the unconquered Army of Northern Virginia, began to roll forward toward Cemetery Hill.

The formation presented a perfect target for Union gunners up on the ridge. Federal artillery opened a murderous fire from the right and left, tearing huge gaps in the Confederate lines and covering the battlefield with bodies and smoke. Forced toward the center by the punishing barrage, the survivors pressed on up the slope. As the Confederates neared their goal, Federal infantrymen opened up a withering musket fire from behind a stone wall at the top of the ridge. On Seminary Ridge, Lee saw a few hundred soldiers briefly make it over the wall and break into the Federal lines before being killed or captured. The survivors drifted back in a broken mass toward the safety of the woods.

Lee rode down to meet his returning men. As he tried to reform shattered units and get them into the safety of the woods, a few raised their hats and gave weak cheers. With evening falling, the field lay silent except for the cries of the wounded. Lee arranged for ambulances and began sketching plans to bring his broken army back across the Potomac. Late that night, standing next to Traveller in the moonlight, Lee suddenly lost his composure. In a shaking voice he said, "I never saw troops behave more magnificently than Pickett's division of Virginians did today in that grand charge upon the enemy. And if they had been supported as they were to have been . . . the day would have been ours." Then he cried out in a voice that rang through the encampment, "Too Bad! Too Bad! Oh! Too Bad!"

The moon shone full upon his massive features and revealed an expression of sadness that I had never before seen on his face.
—JOHN B. IMBODEN
Confederate general, on Lee after the defeat at Gettysburg

7

A Thousand Deaths

On the same day that Lee's shattered divisions drifted down from Cemetery Ridge, the garrison of Vicksburg, Mississippi, surrendered to General Ulysses S. Grant, delivering up to the Federal government the last Confederate-held section of the Mississippi River. The news of Lee's defeat at Gettysburg, coming at the same time as this disaster in the west, shook the faith of the Southern people in the Confederate army and brought a storm of criticism down on Lee. Lee bore the personal abuse patiently as he pulled his broken army back across the Potomac, but he could not endure attacks on the competence of his men. In a letter to Mary he wrote, "The army has laboured hard, endured much, & behaved nobly." Three weeks after the battle, Lee offered his resignation to Davis, who politely refused it.

We must now return to Virginia.
—ROBERT E. LEE

The Confederate line at Petersburg. After the defeat at Gettysburg, Lee's army had no choice but to return to Virginia and defend the Confederate capital, Richmond. His tired, hungry, and ill-shod troops fought valiantly but were soon overpowered by Union forces.

Union gunboats on the Mississippi River fire on the Confederate city of Vicksburg, Mississippi, on July 4, 1863. Some 30,000 Confederate troops surrendered to General Grant at Vicksburg in a Union rout of Southern forces.

Lee did not see his military situation as particularly bad. He had achieved his goal of luring the Army of the Potomac away from Richmond and forcing it to defend Washington, D.C. If he had not managed to deliver a crushing blow, he had at least kept his army in existence as a force that the Federals would have to destroy to win the war. At the end of July, Lee took up a defensive position near the old Chancellorsville battleground on the south bank of the Rapidan River. No sooner had he arrived than the debate began anew over taking away some of his men, this time to help stem an alarming Federal offensive in Tennessee. Lee gave way, and at the beginning of September, Longstreet took 12,000 men of the First Corps and marched west.

After an attempt in early October to see if the old game of getting between the Union army and Washington would work once more, Lee pulled his army back into Orange County, on the south side of the Rapidan, and set up camp for the winter. He and his men were once again faced with cold and starvation as the winter of 1863–64 closed in. He could not get clothes or blankets from Richmond, and his soldiers lived on a few ounces of rancid meat and a handful of meal per day.

Lee's own health mirrored that of his soldiers. The bitter cold weakened him, and a recurrence of the previous year's heart problem kept him off his horse for a month.

When the situation in Tennessee did not improve, Davis asked Lee to take command in the state. But Lee asked to remain in Virginia, though he watched events in the west closely and did not consider himself above offering advice. When the Federals under General Grant broke a Confederate siege of Chattanooga and threatened an advance through Georgia to the Atlantic coast, Davis asked Lee to take command in Georgia to block any such move. But Lee declined.

By March 1864, the Army of the Potomac showed signs of activity. Lee did not fear the 100,000 bluecoats camped on the other side of the Rapidan, but he began to worry about Grant. Grant's star had risen with every western victory until he at last reached the position of commander in chief of all Federal forces. He quickly declared his intent to join Meade's army. On March 24, Confederate spies reported that Grant had arrived in Virginia. Lee did not know much about the new Federal commander, only that he had a reputation for aggressiveness and that he won battles. He asked Davis to return Longstreet's men to the army. Davis agreed, and, a month later, Longstreet's men made camp near Gordonsville, nine miles south of Lee's headquarters. Lee rode down to review his returned troops. An eyewitness reported that as the long lines of ragged troops stood in an open field under a spring sun and cheered their commander, the assembled felt a "bond that held them together. There was no speaking, but the effect was as of a military sacrament." Everyone sensed that the ceremony marked the start of a fight to the finish. After the review, the soldiers crowded around Lee, gently laying their hands on him and on Traveller. The display of affection and trust brought visible tears to Lee's eyes.

On May 4, Grant sent 120,000 men southeast across the Rapidan toward Richmond. Lee could not believe his apparent good fortune when Grant headed straight for the Wilderness. As he ordered the tents struck and directed his 70,000 men east

The overwhelming Union victory at Vicksburg made Ulysses S. Grant a national hero. When Lincoln appointed him commander of all the Union forces in 1864, Grant began to implement a plan to put down the Confederate rebellion once and for all.

to block Grant, Lee felt that he had another Chancellorsville on his hands. Events almost bore him out. The two armies clashed in the Wilderness on May 5, fighting savagely among the brambles, brush, and trees, across soil scattered with bones clad in tattered blue and gray rags that winter storms had washed from their shallow graves. When the battle died down on the evening of May 6, Lee seemed about to cut Grant off from retreat. Everyone on his staff exultantly expected Grant to withdraw. Yet the Federal commander had shown in two days fighting a dogged unwillingness to give up. Lee sensed that Grant would try to shift his army eastward and get between the Army of Northern Virginia and Richmond.

Grant fulfilled Lee's prediction. Instead of retreating, he moved southeast for 10 miles toward the crossroads town of Spotsylvania Court House. Lee had part of the First Corps already in place behind a rapidly growing system of field fortifications when the first Union troops arrived. Grant tried to move Lee by assault, but failed. After two weeks of savage fighting, he tried again, heading for Hanover Junction on the North Anna River. Again he found Lee blocking his path. Despite an intestinal illness that forced him to exchange Traveller for an ambulance wagon, Lee kept anticipating Grant's every move and interposing his men between the Army of the Potomac and Richmond. In each successive attack on Lee's fieldworks, the Union army suffered losses at least twice as great as those of the Confederates, until Grant had lost more men than Lee had in his entire army. Yet Lee knew that he could not in the long run afford this string of defensive victories. Whereas thousands of soldiers that the Confederacy could not replace lay buried between the Wilderness and the North Anna, Grant could draw on an inexhaustible supply of replacements. Far worse, Lee had lost his best officers. James Longstreet had fallen in the Wilderness, seriously wounded by a stray Confederate bullet through the throat. A. P. Hill collapsed from nervous exhaustion at Spotsylvania, and Jeb Stuart fell in a Federal cavalry raid shortly afterward. Lee himself suffered from an in-

> *It was simply bushwhacking on a grand scale, in brush where all formation beyond that of regiments or companies was soon lost and where such a thing as a consistent line of battle on either side was impossible.*
> —Union soldier describing a battle of the Wilderness campaign

testinal seizure that kept him in the ambulance wagon. When one of his aides suggested that the bedridden commander turn the army over to someone else, Lee angrily refused, knowing that with his best officers gone he had to lead his men himself.

In Cold Harbor, only 10 miles northeast of Richmond, the 2 armies clashed again at the beginning of June. After a stunning defeat in which some 7,000 Federal soldiers fell in less than an hour, Grant gave up his frontal-assault strategy and began to look for another solution. While waiting for Grant's next move, Lee received word that Federal forces in the Shenandoah Valley threatened to sweep eastward to join the Army of the Potomac. Lee boldly detached Jubal Early with 8,000 men of the Second Corps to meet the threat, leaving him with fewer than 28,000 infantrymen facing Grant's army.

On June 12, the day that Early marched west, Grant pulled his men out of their trenches and set them marching in a long curve southeast in an effort to cross the James River and get in Lee's rear. This move, if successful, would threaten both the Confederate capital and Lee's army with starvation. The only railroad linking Richmond, and with it the

Grant ordered General William T. Sherman (center) to march his army of some 100,000 men on Atlanta, Georgia, and destroy the city. Sherman, who relished the assignment, cried, "I can make Georgia howl!" as he set off.

Army of Northern Virginia, to North Carolina and the still-surviving sections of the Confederacy ran due south through the city of Petersburg, on the south bank of the Appomattox River. If Grant managed to cut the railroad, Richmond would no longer have an open supply line. On June 16, Grant successfully crossed the James and moved on Petersburg. Lee retreated southward and slipped his army inside the Petersburg fortifications barely in time to save the city.

Grant had finally maneuvered Lee into a position that guaranteed a Federal victory. Lee had 50,000 men to defend the Petersburg lines, which ran in a long curve on the eastern side of the city, anchored at both ends by the Appomattox River, but Grant had more than twice that number. As the weeks passed, Lee pinned his hopes on Early's tiny force off in the valley. The veterans of the Second Corps had driven the Federal army in the valley to seek safety in the mountains. In late June, Early struck out northward in an attempt to threaten or even capture Washington. A success could strengthen the hand of the antiwar party in the North and destroy Lincoln's chances for reelection in the upcoming 1864 election. Early's desperate raid advanced close enough for his men to see Lincoln walking along the Washington defenses, but the men of the Second Corps had to withdraw when Grant hurriedly sent troops to the capital's defense. As the siege continued into the fall of 1864, Grant made a series of assaults on Lee's defenses, drawing his lines ever tighter around Petersburg. In their waterlogged trenches, Lee's men battled disease, ate rotten food, and fought on little sleep.

All across the South, advancing Federal armies seemed about to end forever the dream of Southern independence. The defenders of Petersburg soon learned that every 100-gun salute fired by Union artillery into the city meant another Federal victory. In a desperation move, Davis appointed Lee to the command of the entire Confederate army. Lee appointed Joe Johnston to round up the scattered state and Confederate troops in North Carolina to try to oppose Federal troops marching north from Georgia.

A severe freeze in February struck Lee's poorly clad, ill-fed troops. The bitter cold coupled with desperate letters from home recounting the devastation and suffering caused by the war made many soldiers leave the lines and head for home. Desertion continued at an appalling rate until Lee could field only 1 man for every 20 feet of trenches. On March 2, Lee wrote a letter to General Grant, "desiring to leave nothing untried which may put an end to the calamities of war." He proposed to meet with Grant to negotiate such an end. Grant replied that only Lincoln could discuss ending the war. That same day, Federal cavalry divisions under General Phil Sheridan overwhelmed the last survivors of Early's corps, closing off the Shenandoah Valley forever and leaving him free to join Grant.

In an effort to cut Confederate supply lines, Union soldiers under Sherman's command tear up railroad tracks in Atlanta before beginning their march to the sea. Ted Upson, commander of the 100th Indiana Regiment, said of the resistance met by Sherman's troops, "They might as well try to stop a tornado as Uncle Billy and his boys."

A bomb shelter behind Union lines at Petersburg. When Grant broke through Confederate lines there his forces outnumbered Lee's two-to-one. Lee was forced to lead his spent army back across the Appomattox River, leaving the Confederate capital, Richmond, in Union hands.

The next day, Lee and Davis discussed the available options: to make peace, to attack Grant's army, or to abandon Petersburg and Richmond and try to join the Army of Northern Virginia with Johnston's forces in North Carolina. If Lee could reach Johnston, the two armies together might just defeat Sheridan in time to turn about and face Grant. The last option seemed a slender hope at best. Lee had only 35,000 men fit for duty on the Petersburg and Richmond lines. Johnston had no more than 15,000 in North Carolina. Grant alone had more than 150,000 soldiers facing Lee, with Sheridan's 20,000 soon to join him, while 80,000 headed north from Georgia. Lee could not hope to make such a move until the roads had dried from the winter storms. Davis showed a strong reluctance to abandon Richmond and refused to make any peace with the North that did not include recognition of the South's independence. Lee returned to his headquarters with only one option left—to attack.

On March 25, Lee sent John Gordon with about half of the army on an attack designed to divide Grant's lines in two. The assault failed miserably, largely due to the exhausted state of the men, and left Lee in a weaker position than before. On April 1, Federal cavalry and infantry struck the extreme west end of Lee's lines. The undermanned Confederate defenses snapped, and by evening the line had completely collapsed. The next morning, Grant's troops made an assault along the entire front. Lee lay resting on his couch at headquarters. A knock sounded on the door, and A. P. Hill, still too weak to command, appeared, looking for information on all the firing going on. An hour later, James Longstreet arrived, still recovering from his throat wound but again in command of the First Corps. As dawn came, the three men sat quietly together, the last surviving officers of the Army of Northern Virginia's glory days. Suddenly, one of Lee's aides burst into the room, reporting that he had seen Confederate wagons dashing back toward the city and that Union troops had penetrated far behind the main lines. Hill dashed off with his favorite courier. Lee had no sooner finished dressing when the courier, Sergeant Tucker, appeared, riding Hill's horse. The former commander of the Third Corps had fallen to Federal fire. Lee said hoarsely, his eyes filling with tears, "He is at rest now, and we who are left are the ones to suffer."

Lee had to get his army out of Petersburg. He sent a telegram to Davis declaring his intent to evacuate the city and abandon Richmond. He sent the tattered remnants of his army streaming across the Appomattox River to its north bank; the garrison of Richmond headed southwest to join them. Together the last survivors of the Army of Northern Virginia headed west along the road that would lead finally to Appomattox Courthouse.

Major General Philip Henry Sheridan. What Sherman did to Georgia, Sheridan did to the Shenandoah Valley. After defeating Confederate troops under Jubal Early at Cedar Creek, Sheridan went on a rampage through the valley that effectively eliminated the Army of the Northern Potomac, leaving him free to join Grant in his pursuit of Lee.

8

"Strike the Tent"

As Lee rode back into the Confederate lines from the McLean mansion, the ragged, emaciated soldiers guarding the front began to cheer. One look at Lee's face stopped them cold. The men swarmed around Lee shouting, "General, are we surrendered?" A Confederate officer who clambered atop a wagon wheel to get above the crowd managed to hear Lee reply in a hoarse, barely audible voice, "Men, we have fought the war together, and I have done the best I could for you. You will all be paroled and go to your homes until exchanged. Goodbye." Leaving his soldiers in a state of shock and disbelief, Lee rode to a nearby apple orchard, where he spent most of the day pacing angrily, guarded by his staff from the curious Federal officers who gradually filtered into the Confederate camp. As afternoon began to melt into evening, Lee nerved himself to make the mile-long ride to his tent. A solid wall of cheering men lined both sides of the road. Gaunt and dirty

The war is over. The rebels are our countrymen again.
—ULYSSES S. GRANT
after Lee's surrender at
Appomattox

Lee with his sons Robert, Jr. (right), and Custis. After the war, the aging general was indicted on charges of treason despite the terms agreed upon at Appomattox. Outraged by the bringing of charges against Lee, Grant threatened to resign if his former opponent were brought to trial.

veterans swarmed into the roadway and ran their hands gently over Traveller's flanks as the horse moved on slowly. According to an eyewitness, as Lee passed, "grim-hearted men threw themselves on the ground, covered their faces with their hands and wept like children. Officers of all ranks made no attempt to hide their feelings, but sat on their horses and cried aloud."

Once at his tent, Lee ordered Colonel Marshall to draft a farewell address to the troops. When Marshall returned with the document, Lee struck out a section that he felt might have inflamed continued hatred of the North. The next day he said farewell to his officers, urging all of them to go to their homes and obey the Federal authorities. On April 11, Lee wrote his final report to Davis, his last official act as a Confederate general, and prepared to return home. His troops surrendered their guns and battle flags in a formal ceremony on April 12. Three days later, Lee rode into Richmond, a city devastated by fire and Federal bombardment. As Lee approached his family's rented house on Franklin Street, crowds gathered along the ruined streets and removed their hats in silent homage. Many Federal soldiers did the same. That day, President Lincoln, while attending the theater, was shot and killed by an assassin named John Wilkes Booth.

Richmond after the war. The former Confederate capital was left a burned-out husk after it was overwhelmed and occupied by Union troops. Reconstruction was a painful process made even more painful by the death of Lincoln and infighting in Congress.

With Arlington seized by the government for use as a national cemetery, Lee remained in Richmond, recovering from the stresses of his final campaign. Each day a small crowd of well-wishers gathered silently outside his home. Soldiers who wore both gray and blue came to offer food and help. Lee, however, tried to remain out of the public eye. He recognized with the surrender of his army the practical end of the Confederacy and felt that a speedy acceptance of Union victory would serve the shattered South the best. When a still-active Confederate scout slipped into Richmond and met Lee at a private dinner, Lee told him, "Go home, all you boys who fought with me, and help build up the shattered fortunes of our old state."

Lee worried about the consequences of Lincoln's assassination. Even the most devout partisans of the Southern cause regarded Lincoln's death as a disaster. Lincoln had pressed for clemency toward the seceded states and had managed to hold off those in Congress who were clamoring to punish the South for its rebellion. With Lincoln gone, Lee, along with most Southerners, felt that hope for a peaceful reconstruction of the Union had dimmed. True to the South's expectations, Congress began to implement a reconstruction program designed to punish the Southern states.

With his family home in Arlington turned into a national cemetery, Lee remained in Richmond recovering from his final campaign. There he was visited by soldiers from the North and South. Lee told ex-Confederates, "Go home, all you boys who fought with me, and help build up the shattered fortunes of our old state."

Lee urged Southerners to help rebuild the South rather than flee from the restrictions of Reconstruction. "Virginia has need of all of her sons," he said. Following his own advice, Lee took the job of president of Washington College for $1,500 a year and helped educate Confederate soldiers returning from the war.

In early June, Lee was indicted for treason. He wrote a letter to General Grant expressing his understanding that the terms of his surrender protected him from trial as long as he conformed to them. Lee included with the letter an appeal for pardon to President Andrew Johnson. Grant moved to block the indictment, threatening to resign if ordered to arrest his former opponent, and all charges against Lee were dropped.

Offers of aid poured into the Lee home from admirers and from businessmen eager to capitalize on Lee's fame. A British nobleman offered Lee the lifetime use of an English estate. When an insurance company offered him the then-staggering salary of $50,000 per year for permission to use his name, Lee politely declined.

Finally, on August 4, Lee received an offer he could not refuse. The trustees of Washington College, a small school located in Lexington, Virginia, in the Shenandoah Valley, asked him to serve as president of the college. Lee saw in Washington College the opportunity to earn his living with dignity, lending his prestige and experience to an institution that would appreciate it. Moreover, he believed that he would be making a real contribution to the rebuilding of the South by teaching the young soldiers coming home from the bloody battlefields.

Washington College needed all the help Lee could give it. The war that had raged up and down the Shenandoah Valley had left its buildings almost in ruins, and at the time of Lee's arrival in mid-September, the college could boast only 4 professors and 40 students. Lee went straight to work, becoming in the words of the historian Eugene Smith, "at once president, dean, director of college development, adviser to the faculty, registrar, purchasing agent and supervisor of grounds," all at a salary of $125 per month. He gave the student body, a mixture of 17-year-old boys and older Confederate veterans trying to find their feet again after 4 years of military life, the same personal attention that he had given his cadets at West Point. He reviewed individual test scores and invited students who did poorly into his office for a talk, putting them at ease with the same relaxing charm that had marked his receptions at the military academy. He wrote a constant stream of letters to worried parents, keeping them abreast of their sons' progress. He abolished the college's rigid classical curriculum in favor of an elective course of study that students could tailor to their own needs. Following his own conviction that education would best help the South recover and move into the modern world, Lee added courses in business, banking, and agriculture and prompted Washington College to offer the first course in journalism ever offered by an American college. He also tried to instill a sense of duty and honor in his students. When a new arrival asked for a copy of the college rules, the former commander of the Army of Northern Virginia replied, "Young gentleman, we have no printed rules. We have but one rule here, and it is that every student must be a gentleman."

Lee soon settled into a daily routine that the townspeople could set their clocks by — a morning of office work, followed by dinner and an afternoon ride on Traveller into the nearby mountains. When the trustees made Lee's house habitable, Mrs. Lee and her three daughters moved up from Richmond.

Lee adored his daughters. His need for them extended to the point, however, that he could not stand to share their affections with anyone else. He made it clear that he did not want them to marry, but rather to remain forever at home to take care of him and of their mother. Though not without complaint, they obeyed their father's wishes and never married.

During Lee's tenure, the student body of Washington College jumped from 40 to 400 and began to include students from throughout the country. Also, more professors joined the faculty to teach new courses in chemistry, metallurgy, architecture, engineering, and modern languages. Lee oversaw the construction of new buildings, including a new library and a new chapel. He began to enjoy his new job as he had no other since he began his military career. Finding such pleasure in civilian life, he once commented that he believed he had made the greatest mistake of his life by attending West Point.

I would die; yes I would die willingly because I love my country. But if this war is ever over, I'll be damned if I ever love another country!
—Confederate soldier

In 1870, Lee and his daughter Agnes toured the South. Surprised by the droves of cheering Southerners who turned out to greet their hero, the humble Lee remarked, "Why should they care to see me? I am only an old Confederate."

Lee remained quiet about the war, appearing totally disinterested in the scramble of other Confederate veterans to claim credit for victories or place blame for defeat. With Lexington far off the beaten path, few of his old comrades saw him. Those that did were shocked by Lee's appearance. He looked 20 years beyond his age, and the fierce combativeness that had sustained him and his subordinates in battle had died, leaving only the fatigue of 4 years of bloody war.

The Southern people, however, refused to let Lee fade into obscurity. For them, he was a hero. But Lee had no ambition for further national prominence. He turned a deaf ear to calls for him to run for governor of Virginia, dismissed calls for the Democratic party to nominate him for the Presidential elections of 1868 as pure lunacy, and contented himself with running the college, editing the memoirs of his father, and writing letters to his former subordinates asking for material to write a history of the Army of Northern Virginia.

As the decade waned, so did Lee's health. He found walking increasingly difficult and had trouble enduring Traveller's brisk trot. Any exercise caused increasing pain in his chest. His old dignified carriage disappeared, and his shoulders sagged. Lee began to call himself an invalid and spoke of resigning from the college presidency. In the spring of 1870, the college faculty pressed him to take a vacation and suggested that he take a tour of the South. Lee reluctantly agreed to go if Agnes would accompany him.

On March 24, 1870, he and his daughter departed, intending to travel through the South as ordinary tourists. An incredulous Confederate veteran spotted them four days into their journey in Warrenton, North Carolina, and invited them to spend the night with his family. When the two boarded a train the next day for Augusta, Georgia, the news of their trip raced out ahead of them. Huge crowds congregated at station stops along Lee's route chanting, "Lee! Lee!" Bands played, and local dignitaries, including some Federal officers, vied with each other in their efforts to pay Lee homage. Lee, remaining out of sight as much as possible, found the uproar puzzling. "Why should they care to see me?" he asked. "I am only a poor old Confederate." As the tour progressed through Georgia, Florida, and back into the Carolinas, the supposedly restful vacation became an exhausting triumphal procession that quickly drained Lee of his last feeble reserves of strength. When he reached his son Rooney's plantation on the Peninsula in Virginia, his wife found him weak and exhausted and quickly brought him back to Lexington.

As the summer progressed, Lee found himself too ill to ride Traveller. Nonetheless, he went about business as usual when fall classes resumed. On September 28, after his usual morning schedule, he attended a meeting at his local church. When he returned home for tea in the afternoon, he suddenly paused and sank silently into his chair with a strange look on his face. His wife instantly sent for doctors. For two weeks, Lee lay in bed, his wife and daughters constantly by his side. For a time, he seemed to improve, eating well and able to speak softly. On October 11, however, he fell into a delirium, his mind wandering back to wartime as he gave orders once again to his officers. At one point he burst out, "Tell Hill he must come up!" The next morning, Lee briefly roused and said, "Strike the tent." He died shortly afterward.

As the years passed and the states of the former Confederacy finally rejoined the Union under their own governments, Robert E. Lee became a figure of epic proportions for not only the South but for the entire nation. He symbolized the last flowering of the ancient chivalric ideals of duty, honor, and silent fortitude in defeat. The Army of Northern Virginia became widely regarded as the finest American army to ever see combat and a source of pride for the entire American military.

However, the qualities that earned Lee his greatest fame may have contributed most to his ultimate failure. His sense of loyalty and duty to Virginia led him to override his own feelings and fight a war whose roots at heart he bitterly opposed and one that could not have, in the face of a determined Northern effort, ultimately succeeded. The excessive courtliness and respect for the feelings of others

Thousands line up at the chapel on the campus of Washington College to pay their last respects to General Robert Edward Lee, who perhaps more than any one man came to personify the dignity, honor, courage, and, ultimately, the defeat of the South. A year after Lee's death, the name of the college was changed to Washington and Lee University as a tribute to its former president.

that first surfaced in the mountains of West Virginia and rose again with possibly disastrous effect in the face of Longstreet's insubordination at Gettysburg had no place in a mostly volunteer, half-trained army fighting a revolutionary civil war. Lee's combative nature, which drove him to strike a blow while the strength to do so remained, wasted lives at Malvern Hill and possibly ruined his army at Gettysburg.

Nonetheless, Lee's career displayed a constant effort to remain true to his ideals, even in defeat. His constant efforts to convince his people to accept the judgment of war and to hold no grudge against the North helped make the American Civil War unique in history. In no other civil war has the vanquished side laid down its arms and peacefully gone home, to turn the memories of its struggle into a proud legend that it could share with its conquerors rather than into a source of unending bitterness and divisive hatred. Faced with the spiritual leadership of his people, Lee chose to use his power to help reunite his divided country.

In the 1970s a government clerk in Washington D.C. discovered a yellowed scrap of paper while searching through an old filing cabinet. Dated October 2, 1865, the paper read:

> I Robert E. Lee of Lexington, Virginia do solemnly swear, in the presence of Almighty God, that I will henceforth support, protect, and defend the Constitution of the United States, and the Union of the States thereunder, and that I will, in like manner, abide by and faithfully support all laws and proclamations which have been made during the existing rebellion with reference to the emancipation of slaves, so help me God.

Lee's loyalty oath, taken to fulfill the requirements made by the Federal government for Confederate officers to return to U.S. citizenship, had apparently been suppressed and hidden to make him appear unrepentant. The U.S. House of Representatives acted on Lee's oath in July 1975, after a delay of 110 years, and voted to restore him to full citizenship in the United States.

Further Reading

Anderson, Nancy S., and Dwight Anderson. *The Generals.* New York: Knopf, 1988.

Baines, Rae. *Robert E. Lee: Brave Leader.* Mahwah, NJ: Troll Associates, 1985.

Brandt, Keith. *Robert E. Lee.* Mahwah, NJ: Troll Associates, 1985.

Bruns, Roger. *Abraham Lincoln.* New York: Chelsea House, 1986.

Catton, Bruce. *The Civil War.* New York: Houghton Mifflin, 1987.

———. *The Coming Fury.* Garden City, NY: Doubleday, 1961.

———. *Never Call Retreat.* Garden City, NY: Doubleday, 1965.

———. *Terrible Swift Sword.* Garden City, NY: Doubleday, 1963.

Davis, Burke. *To Appomattox.* New York: Holt, Rinehart & Winston, 1959.

Dowdey, Clifford. *Lee.* Boston: Little, Brown, 1965.

Frassanito, William A. *Grant & Lee: The Virginia Campaigns.* New York: Scribners, 1983.

King, Perry Scott. *Jefferson Davis.* New York: Chelsea House, 1990.

Lee, Robert E., Jr. *My Father, General Lee.* Garden City, NY: Doubleday, 1960.

Malone, Dumas, and Basil Rauch. *Crisis of the Union: 1841–1877.* Englewood Cliffs, NJ: Prentice-Hall, 1960.

Monsell, Helen A. *Robert E. Lee: Young Confederate.* New York: Bobbs-Merrill, 1983.

O'Brien, Steven. *Ulysses S. Grant.* New York: Chelsea House, 1991.

Sanborne, Margaret. *Robert E. Lee.* Vols. 1 & 2. New York: Lippincott, 1967.

Smith, Eugene. *Lee and Grant: A Dual Biography.* New York: McGraw-Hill, 1984.

Smith, Page. *Trial by Fire: A People's History of the Civil War and Reconstruction.* New York: Penguin Books, 1982.

Weidhorn, Manfred. *Robert E. Lee.* New York: Macmillan, 1988.

Zadra, Dan. *Statesmen in America: Robert E. Lee.* Mankato, MN: Creative Education, 1988.

Chronology

Jan. 19, 1807	Born Robert Edward Lee at Stratford Hall, Westmoreland County, Virginia, the fourth child of Henry "Light-Horse Harry" Lee and Ann Carter Lee
1810	Lee family forced to leave Stratford, moves to Alexandria, Virginia
1825–29	Lee attends U.S. Military Academy at West Point; graduates second in class
June 1831	Marries Mary Custis
Aug. 1846	Ordered to Texas to join army marching on Mexico shortly after outbreak of Mexican War
May 1852	Returns to West Point as the military academy's ninth superintendent
Oct. 1859	John Brown raids federal arsenal at Harpers Ferry, Virginia; Lee puts down the insurrection
Jan. 1861	First Southern states begin to secede from the Union
April 1861	Fort Sumter attacked by Confederate naval forces; Civil War begins; Lee resigns from U.S. Army
July 1861	First Battle of Manassas; Lee sent to western Virginia to coordinate Confederate defense
March 1862	Lee recalled to Richmond as commander in chief of all Confederate forces under President Jefferson Davis
Aug. 28–30, 1862	Second Battle of Manassas
Sept. 1862	Battle of Antietam; President Abraham Lincoln issues the Emancipation Proclamation
Dec. 13, 1862	Battle of Fredericksburg
May 1–4, 1863	Battle of Chancellorsville
July 1–3, 1863	Battle of Gettysburg
July 3, 1863	Ulysses S. Grant captures Vicksburg, Mississippi
March 24, 1864	Grant joins the Army of the Potomac
May 5–6, 1864	Battle of the Wilderness
June 18, 1864	Siege of Petersburg begins
April 2, 1865	Lee's lines break at Petersburg; final retreat of the Army of Northern Virginia begins
April 1865	Lee surrenders to Grant at Appomattox Courthouse; returns to Richmond; President Lincoln is assassinated
Sept. 1865	Lee takes position as president of Washington College, Lexington, Virginia
Oct. 2, 1865	Signs loyalty oath to the United States
Oct. 12, 1870	Dies in Lexington
July 1975	Lee's citizenship restored by U.S. House of Representatives

Index

Warren Brown holds a B.A. in history and literature from Tufts University and studied music at the New England Conservatory of Music in Boston. A freelance writer and former Fulbright scholar who has a special interest in the Civil War, his other books for Chelsea House include *The Search for the Northwest Passage* and *Roald Amundsen and the Quest for the South Pole.*

Arthur M. Schlesinger, jr., taught history at Harvard for many years and is currently Albert Schweitzer Professor of the Humanities at City University of New York. He is the author of numerous highly praised works in American history and has twice been awarded the Pulitzer Prize. He served in the White House as special assistant to Presidents Kennedy and Johnson.